Academic Writing Strategies:

Yasuo Nakatani

Focus on Global Issues for Sustainable Development Goals

KINSEIDO

Kinseido Publishing Co., Ltd.

3-21 Kanda Jimbo-cho, Chiyoda-ku,
Tokyo 101-0051, Japan

First published 2020 by Kinseido Publishing Co., Ltd.

Cover design   Takayuki Minegishi
Text design   C-leps Co., Ltd.

Photos
p. 29 © Cowardlion | Dreamstime.com, p. 49 © Jeffplay | Dreamstime.com, p. 59 (top) © Chris Dorney |
Dreamstime.com, p. 71 © Chris Dorney | Dreamstime.com, p.101 © Spongecake | Dreamstime.com
p. 124, courtesy of Yamaha Motor Co., Ltd.

The United Nations Sustainable Development Goals website:
https://www.un.org/sustainabledevelopment/
The content of this publication has not been approved by the United Nations and
does not reflect the views of the United Nations or its officials or Member States.

🎧 音声ファイル無料ダウンロード

http://www.kinsei-do.co.jp/download/4109

この教科書で 🎧 DL 00 の表示がある箇所の音声は、上記 URL または QR コードにて
無料でダウンロードできます。自習用音声としてご活用ください。

▶ PC からのダウンロードをお勧めします。スマートフォンなどでダウンロードされる場合は、
　 ダウンロード前に**「解凍アプリ」をインストール**してください。
▶ URL は、**検索ボックスではなくアドレスバー (URL 表示欄)** に入力してください。
▶ お使いのネットワーク環境によっては、ダウンロードできない場合があります。

◎ CD 00　左記の表示がある箇所の音声は、教室用 CD（Class Audio CD）に収録されています。

はじめに

本書では、学習者にとって関心のある執筆テーマを SDGs（持続可能な開発目標）から選ぶことで社会問題への認識を深め、そこから身についた自分の考えを英文でまとめる練習を行います。本書は 3 つのパートから成り、Part 1 ではまず、読者にとって読みやすいパラグラフを書く基本を学びます。Part 2 では、自分の考えをより具体的に記述する方法を学びます。そして Part 3 では、エッセイの書き方や、論文執筆に向けた基礎を学びます。

・英文エッセイでは問題解決能力が身についているのかを試される

世界の大学生に求められているのは未来のリーダーになることです。これは企業のトップや政治家になることだけではありません。環境問題や貧困の問題など世の中にあふれている様々な課題を自ら進んで解決していくことです。このために欧米の授業では、各自が課題を見つけ解決する能力を求められます。この過程でエッセイを書くことで、事象を適切に把握し、問題を分析して独自の解答を提示するトレーニングとなります。

・英米の大学で必要なのは英文エッセイを書く力

留学のための IELTS や TOEFL でも特定のテーマが与えられ、それに対する問題解決能力が試されます。現地に留学した場合は、当然のことながら授業ごとに多くのエッセイを書くことになります。このテキストは、エッセイを書くのに効果的なストラテジーを基礎から学びます。英米の大学へ留学を希望する人や、いずれ英語で卒業論文を書く人、将来英語を使い活躍したい人に着実にライティング力が身につくように構成されています。本書は IELTS の Task 2 や TOEFL の Task 2 で取り扱う問題解決のエッセイにも対応しています。

・持続可能な開発目標（SDGs: Sustainable Development Goals）の課題に向き合う

そもそも社会問題への興味が少ない、課題に対する認識があまりないと英文エッセイは書けません。本書では、国連が提唱した世界的な課題である SDGs の中から日本の大学生にとって身近な問題をテーマとして扱います。様々な重要な問題を把握し、解決方法を考えることで次第に学習者の問題意識を高めていきます。ライティングのトレーニングを通して、明確に自分の意見を述べられることを目指します。

本書の特徴

□ **毎回学習者にとって関心のある興味深いテーマについて書く**

英文エッセイは社会の課題に対して、意見を述べたり解決方法を示すことが主な目的の一つです。本書は SDGs の中から身近なテーマを選び社会問題への認識を深め、自分の考えを英文でまとめるトレーニングを行います。

□ **より説得力のある英文を書くためのストラテジーを学ぶ**

読者にとって読みやすく説得力のあるパラグラフや、エッセイ構築に必要な理論的原則をわかりやすく解説します。文書の流れの作り方や、読者の効果的な誘導の仕方を、最初はパターン練習から始め、次第に自由に使いこなし英文が書けるようになります。

□ **豊富なコーパス・データに基づく実際に使用される効果的例文の提示**

欧米の大学の英語母語話者が書いたエッセイ、英国大学入試 A レベル、さらに TOEFL、IELTS の検定試験の模範解答を収集し約 200 万語のコーパスを構築しました。この大量のデータから使用頻度の高い語彙・フレーズを抽出し活用しています。これらを活用して英文の読みやすさを構築するストラテジーの習得を目指します。これまでの英文ライティングの理論を、コーパス分析で確認した、重要な表現や例文を通して学んでいきます。

□ **ライティングで間違いやすいエラーを解説**

各章の最後で取り組む Focus on Accuracy では、英文添削で数多くみられるエラーの解決方法を説明しています。これらエラーの修正項目を意識して改善できることを目指します。毎回、書いた英文をこの項目に沿って自己添削していき、特定のエラー改善への認識を高めます。

□ **ピアレビューやグループワークを通して読者を意識する**

書く目的は読者を説得することです。この目的のもと、学習者同士が書かれた英文の読み手となり、ともに課題に取り組みます。毎回、感想を書き Focus on Accuracy の各項目を互いに確認します。また各章で提示された課題に対して学習同士で対話を行い、問題解決の提案方法を身につけます。

□ **語彙の多様性、読者の誘導、誤用の削減に役立つ資料**

Writing Tip by Corpus Analysis（全 3 回）では、コーパス分析で得られた、英文エッセイで使用頻度の高い語彙の書き換え、読者の誘導に有効なメタディスコースのまとめ、誤用の多い語彙などを参考として掲載しています。

本書の使い方

各章の最初のページでは、書き始める準備を行います。

・トピック／ SDGs ／写真

各章のライティングの課題の大まかなポイントを把握します。また、毎回課題を連想させる関連写真を掲載していますので、話題に関連するスキーマを活性化させるアドバンスオーガナイザーとなります。

・Pre-Task

クラスメイトと各章の課題に関連する話題を話し合い、書き始める準備をします。

・Strategic Points

ここでアカデミックライティングのストラテジーの項目が示されています。

・この章で学ぶこと

各レッスンの要点をまとめています。

次のページ以降では、実際にタスクに取り組んでいきます。

・Strategic Focus

ストラテジーの中心となる概念を日本語で理解します。

・Task 1

導入のタスクです。Strategic Focus に関連したタスクからクラスメイトと話し合ったり、書き始めたりします。

・Writing Strategy

具体的なライティングストラテジーの重要事項を日本語で理解します。

・Task 2 ～

Writing Strategy の説明事項の内容を理解するためのタスクです。

▶ Group Work

クラスメイトとペアワークまたは少人数のグループワークで、英語によるインタラクションを行い、話し合う機会を通してライティングの内容の理解を深めます。

・ Task for Output

各章の課題に対する英文のパラグラフやエッセイを書くタスクです。Scaffolding Approach により、最初は定型に沿った形で書き始め、次第に定型を外し、自然に長い英文が書けるように工夫しています。ここでも、Group Work を含め、以下のような活動を行います。

▶ Template

課題の形式ごとに、パラグラフやエッセイ・論文の形式をまとめています。これをそのまま活用し、書く内容の設計図を作ります。

▶ Write It Down

実際にパラグラフを書きます。

▶ Self-editing

書いた英文が Writing Strategy の観点で適切に書かれているかを自分で点検し添削します。何回もこの活動に取り組むことで特定のストラテジーに意識を高め、英文の正確さを高めていきます。

▶ Peer Review

つねに読者を意識して、読みやすい英文を書くために、自己添削が終わった時点でクラスメイトに確認して添削してもらいます。また書いたものにコメントや意見をもらうことで、書く目標や達成感を持たせます。学習者同士の意識を高め、英文の正確性を向上させます。

・ Focus on Accuracy

英文を書く際に間違いやすくエラーの多いポイントを解説しています。正確な英文を書く際の参照となります。

・ Writing Tip by Corpus Analysis（全3回）

英文エッセイを集めたエッセイコーパスの特徴語で、特に使用頻度の高い語彙表現をまとめています。英文の多様性を改善する際の参照となります。

Table of Contents

Academic Writing Strategies

Focus on Global Issues for Sustainable Development Goals

Strategic Points	Focus on Accuracy
End focus strategy, End weight strategy	Punctuation 1
Creating unity, Topic sentence, Supporting sentence, Example	Punctuation 2
Grammatical cohesion, Vocabulary cohesion, Creating variety of vocabulary	Determiner and Article 1
Raising awareness of readers, Use of metadiscourse	Determiner and Article 2
Hedges, Boosters	Subject-Verb Agreement

Brainstorming, Idea listing, Clustering, Organizing ideas, Critical thinking	Hedges
Attracting audience, Topic and controlling ideas	Modal Verbs
Developing supporting sentences, Enhancing coherence by supporting the topic sentence	Quantifiers
Closing a paragraph, Enhancing reader's understanding	Infinitives or Gerunds
Three different types of comparison and contrast paragraphs	Noun Usage

Introduction, Body, Conclusion, Thesis statement	Use of Adjectives and Adverbs
Providing solutions and relating benefits	Conditionals
Introduction Move 1: Defining your research territory	Literature Review
Introduction Move 2: Creating a research niche Introduction Move 3: Occupying the niche	Tense
Enhancing reader-centered strategies	

Writing Tip by Corpus Analysis 1, 2, 3 ·········027/036/119

Part 1

Basic Strategies for Paragraph Writing

Part I では読者にとって読みやすいパラグラフを
書く基本を学びます。

Topic: Healthy Food

3 GOOD HEALTH AND WELL-BEING

Ensure healthy lives and promote well-being for all at all ages.

Chapter 1
Flow of Sentences

■ **Pre-Task :** Talk with your classmates about your favorite dishes.

☑ **Strategic Points** ···End focus strategy
End weight strategy

In this chapter you will learn how to enhance reader-centered strategies for paragraph writing. The focus is on the information structure of each sentence to create the flow of sentences.

▶ この章で学ぶこと ▶ 読者が読みやすい英文の基礎
▶ 英文の流れの作り方

Strategic Focus 1: Creating Flow of Sentences

アカデミック・ライティングでは、reader-centered と呼ばれる「読者中心」を意識した、読みやすい英文を書く必要があります。そのためには英文の流れ（flow of sentences）を構築します。

Task 1

次の英文はどちらが読みやすいですか。また、その理由を考えて答えなさい。

a. You can see some local people cooking their meals in traditional ways. Their ancestors created the traditions.

b. You can see some local people cooking their meals in traditional ways. The traditions were created by their ancestors.

▶ **Clue**　aとbの英文の流れの違いは？

・Your answer: **a / b**

・Reason: _____

_____

Writing Strategy 1　Position of Words

英文はテーマ（theme）と呼ばれる主部と、リーム（rheme）と呼ばれる述部で構成されています。テーマには伝える話題を、リームにはその話題の内容について書きます。

例1　
　　　　テーマ　　　　　リーム

　この英文の話題は、一般的な「日本人」に関することで、内容は「彼らが伝統的な食事を楽しんでいる」ということになります。このように、通常は文の前方にあるテーマで伝えたい話題を読者に示し、リームでテーマの説明を書きます。また、テーマには読者が知っている「既知」情報を、リームには読者の知らない「新規」の情報を置くと読みやすくなります。

　それでは例2を見てください。例1の英文に続く2文目に注目し、既知情報と新規情報を確認しましょう。

例2　Japanese enjoy their traditional cuisine. It consists of well-balanced foods.

この英文の情報の配置は次のようになります。１文目の最後にある their traditional cuisine と２文目の文頭にある代名詞 It は同じ情報です。つまり２文目は、読者にとって既知の情報から始まっています。このため１文目の終わりから２文目にスムーズに読むことができます。これを<u>文の結束（cohesion）</u>と言います。

Japanese enjoy their traditional cuisine.

It consists of well-balanced foods.
既知　　　　　　　　　新規

　また、２文目の最後にある well-balanced foods が新規の情報になります。読者は、続く文はこの内容に関することが来ることを予想します。このように、文末にある「新しい重要な情報」に焦点をあてることを、<u>エンド・フォーカス（end focus）</u>と呼びます。

Task 2

次の英文のテーマとリームを分析し、２文目の既知の情報を○で囲み、新規の情報に下線を引きなさい。

1. I think cooking is a great tradition. It helps people to relax.
2. The use of technological advancements makes preparing food much easier for mothers. It helps those who work outside the home a great deal.

▶ **Attention!**　文頭の既知情報による結束は、前文の文末でなくて他の部分でもよい。

■ **Group Work:** Talk with your classmates.
なぜ文末に新しい重要な情報を置くと読みやすいのでしょうか。

Writing Strategy 2 ▶ End Weight Strategy

文末に同じような情報が並ぶ際は、音節の多い情報を後ろに持ってくると読みやすくなります。

　次の英文 a, b では、文末に chips と chocolate という同列の情報が並んでいます。このような場合は、音節の多い chocolate を後ろに置いた a の英文の方が読みやすくなります。

a. Many children go for **chips** and **chocolate**.
b. Many children go for **chocolate** and **chips**.

Task 3

次の英文を読みやすく書き換えなさい。

1. Movie stars live extravagant lifestyles with gorgeous houses and cars.

_____

_____

2. If you join our cooking club, you will have the chance to attend free master classes and events.

_____

_____

Writing Strategy 3   The Position of Phrases

文頭や文末のどちらにも置ける句は、読みやすさを実現するために、書き手が位置を選びます。

次の英文に続ける場合、a と b ではどちらが読みやすいでしょうか。

People have to work under somebody's supervision in many workplaces.
 a. Employees cannot choose their boss in most cases.
 b. In most cases, employees cannot choose their boss.

答えは、b の英文です。理由は In most cases という句を文頭に置いた方が、下の例文のように、前文の文末の内容と結びつきやすくなるからです。

People have to work under somebody's supervision in many workplaces.

In most cases, employees cannot choose their boss.

Task 4

読みやすい英文にするために、2文目を書き換えなさい。

This issue seems to have been caused by farming methods used 30 years ago. Pigs were given modified gene feed in this country in the 1980s and 1990s.

_____

_____

Writing Strategy **4** The Position of Clause

句と同様に、節も読みやすいように主節と従属節の配置を選びます。下の例文の２文目の If 節は、後方に置き most children の節から始めることも可能です。しかし、If 節を前に置くことにより、these relationships という１文目にある既知情報から始まり結束ができます。

Relationships between parents and children play an essential role in a child's success in school.

If these relationships are well-developed, most children tend to trust their teachers.

─Task 5 ─

読みやすい英文にするために、２文目を書き換えなさい。

We are surrounded by restaurants selling unhealthy foods at low prices. Children would not be tempted to buy take-away food if there were fewer of these shops.

─Task 6 ─

次のパラグラフの２文目以降の既知情報を○で囲み、新規情報に下線を引きなさい。

Model Paragraph 1

Several medical experts point out that children are overweight and the situation is getting worse. This problem is affected by lifestyle changes at home. Some parents are too busy to spend time cooking decent food. They tend to choose meals which need little time to prepare. Due to this sort of situation, there is an increase in the amount of processed food that children eat at home. They may not have as much fresh food and vegetables as previous generations had.

Task for Output 1

Model Paragraph 1 に関して、次の 1 ～ 4 に答えなさい。

1. Do you agree or disagree with the claim of the model paragraph?

I agree / disagree _____

_____

2. Why do you agree or disagree?

_____

3. Can you think of any evidence or examples to support your idea?

_____

4. Put the above three sentences together, focusing on the flow of sentences. Use Template 1 for reference.

Template 1 ■ Writing a Short Comment for Agree or Disagree	
賛成・反対を述べる	I agree / disagree ...
理由を述べる	This is because ...
具体例を述べる	For example ...

_____

_____

_____

_____

■ *Peer Review:* Check your peer's writing.

4 でまとめた英文に結束があるか、既知と新規の情報はどれか、ペアになって確認しなさい。

Task for Output 2

Model Paragraph 2

Japanese foods are getting more and more popular. They are very tasty and ingredients are well-balanced. Traditionally, people use fresh seasonal ingredients that can be obtained only at specific times of the year. Some food should be very fresh and you should go to the market on a daily basis. For example, sushi is made with raw fish which contains a lot of vitamins and protein. Having such ideal dishes enables people to stay healthy. That may be one of the reasons why Japanese have a long life expectancy.

Model Paragraph 2 で述べられている内容に賛成か反対か、自分の意見を 3 ～ 4 文の英語で書きなさい。理由やその裏付けとなる具体例も書きなさい。 ▶ **Template 1** [p. 7]

_____

_____

_____

_____

◼ *Self-editing*
英文に結束ができているか確認しなさい。

◼ *Peer Review:* Check your peer's writing.
1. 英文に結束があるか、既知と新規の情報をお互いに確認しなさい。
2. それぞれの意見を読んで英語で感想を書きなさい。

_____

_____

_____

_____

▶ *Clue*　誰かの意見にコメントをする表現
　　 I think you have a point ...　　I understand your opinion ...

Task for Output 3
自分の好きな食べ物について、理由やその具体例を英語で書きなさい。

_____

_____

_____

_____

句読点 1

■ ピリオド［.］

　文の終わりを読者に示すのがピリオドです。「止まれ」の合図となるので、読者はその前で読むスピードを遅くします。ピリオドがない英文は run-on sentence と呼ばれ、読者は読み続けるため、意味の理解が困難になります。

Quiz 1 ｜ 次の英文を読みやすく書き換えなさい。

Children these days get very little exercise they do not play outside they play video games at home

_____

_____

■ コンマ［,］

　コンマは1つの区切りを示します。代表的なものに次のような種類があります。

1. 文頭のコンマ：文頭に置いて、後に続く節に情報を加えます。

　　例　First, I point out the benefits of fresh food.

　　　　Accordingly, Japanese food is healthy.

2. 並列のコンマ：語句や、句、節などを並べる際にコンマで区切ります。

　　例　Visitors love some Japanese food, such as sushi, tempura, and sukiyaki.

　　　　If you come tomorrow, you can get nice fish.

3. 挿入のコンマ：文中に語句などを挿入したい時に使います。

　　例　British desserts, on the contrary, are very rich.

　　　　There is another factor, however, which contributes to the bad condition.

Quiz 2 ｜ 次の英文をコンマを加えて書き換えなさい。

After coming back home I usually start cooking.

_____

On weekends, he plays tennis football and basketball.

_____

Topic: Food Issues

12 RESPONSIBLE CONSUMPTION AND PRODUCTION

Ensure sustainable consumption and production patterns.

Chapter 2
Basic Paragraph

■ **Pre-Task :** Talk with your classmates about food problems.

☑ **Strategic Points** ··· Creating unity
  Topic sentence
  Supporting sentence
  Example

   In this chapter you will learn how to organize a paragraph. The focus is on the basic structure of a paragraph and the role of individual sentences.

▶ この章で学ぶこと ▶ パラグラフの基本構成
         ▶ パラグラフの統一性の作り方

Strategic Focus 2: Developing a Basic Paragraph

英文ライティングではパラグラフが情報伝達の基本となります。1つのパラグラフでは1つのトピックについて書きます。これを<u>パラグラフの統一性（unity）</u>と呼びます。

━Task 1━

次の英文には unity がありますか。もしなければ、どのように修正すべきか答えなさい。

　　Because of recent technology, preparation of food has become easier. It helps mothers to spend less time on household chores. Using a washing machine is another good way. However, there are some problems with nutrition due to the sudden rise in processed and canned foods. They often contain a lot of salt and sugar.

▶ **Clue**　パラグラフの内容が、すべて1つのトピックに関連するものか確認する。

Writing Strategy **5**　Creating Unity

・異なるトピックについて書く場合は、新しいパラグラフを始めます。
・パラグラフの内容を伝える <u>topic sentence（トピックセンテンス）</u>で始めると読みやすくなります。
・1つのパラグラフでは topic sentence で記述したことだけについて書きます。

以下は topic sentence の基本構造です。

テーマ	リーム
トピック （＝パラグラフの話題）	話題の展開 （＝話題をどのように伝えるか）

以下の topic sentence の話題と、その展開を見てみましょう。

例　

このパラグラフの話題は「自宅での調理」についてです。話題の展開は、「その利点について書く」ことが読者に伝えられます。これ以外の話題について書きたい時はパラグラフを変えることになります。

■ *Group Work:* Talk with your classmates.

次の各英文は topic sentence です。トピックと話題の展開を確認し、後の文にはどのような内容が続くのか話し合いなさい。

1. Chinese food has a variety of flavors.

2. Some foods at convenience stores contain unhealthy ingredients.

Writing Strategy **6**   Basic Paragraph Structure

基本のパラグラフは以下の３つの要素で構成されます。このように、読者を効果的に誘導するための情報の流れの型を Move（ムーヴ）と呼びます。

1. Topic sentence: パラグラフの話題と展開

2. Supporting sentence: topic sentence をサポートする内容

3. Example: サポートする具体例

基本のパラグラフは以下の逆三角形のように、一般的な話題から詳細な例へと、より具体的な Move を構築することで読みやすくなります。

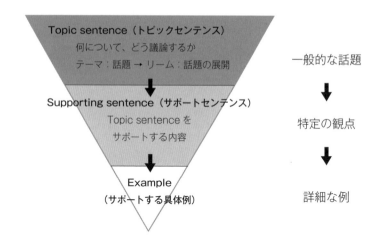

━Task 2 ━

次の英文のパラグラフの構成を説明しなさい。また、Chapter 1 で学習した各文の結束（cohesion）も確認しなさい。

Cooking at home has some benefits for family members. They can share precious time. For example, they go shopping and prepare dinner together.

Task for Output 1

Model Paragraph 1

 DL 04  CD04

When you are busy, fast food is very convenient and not too expensive. If you have a short lunch break, all you need to do is to visit a hamburger chain outlet and pick up a reasonable set menu. You can eat in or take away a meal in a short time. When you are too busy for cooking, you can take your children to a shop which has tempting menu selections for kids. They love sweet drinks and French fries and never complain about strong flavors. As long as you do not eat fast food too often, it may be a good way to manage your time and money.

Model Paragraph 1 に関して、次の 1 ～ 4 に答えなさい。

1. What do you think about this issue?

In my opinion, _____

2. Why do you think so?

Because _____

3. Any examples or evidence?

For example, _____

4. Put the above three sentences together, focusing on the flow of sentences.

Template 2 ■ Writing a Short Opinion	
意見を述べる	In my opinion, ... / I believe ...
理由を述べる	This is because ...
具体例を述べる	For example, ...

_____

_____

_____

_____

■ *Peer Review:* Check your peer's writing.

4 でまとめた英文に結束があるか、既知と新規の情報はどれか、ペアになって確認しなさい。

Writing Strategy **7** Writing a Short Comment

短い賛成・反対のコメントを書く際には、最低2～3文で Move を作ります。

  1. Topic sentence: 自分の意見

   e.g. I agree with your point ... / Your opinion is very convincing ...

  2. Supporting sentence: その理由や根拠

   e.g. This is because ... / In particular, it is true that ...

賛成・反対を述べる際に役立つ表現

■**賛成の時**　Your opinion is very clear ...

　　　　　　I agree with your point ...

■**反対の時**　It may be difficult to say that ...

　　　　　　It is not always true ...

　　　　　　I see your point, but ...

💾 *Peer Work*

Task for Output 1 の4でまとめたペアの英文を読み、短いコメントを書きなさい。

Your opinion is ＿＿＿＿＿＿＿＿＿＿＿＿＿＿＿＿＿＿＿＿＿＿＿＿＿＿＿

This is because ＿＿＿＿＿＿＿＿＿＿＿＿＿＿＿＿＿＿＿＿＿＿＿＿＿＿

For example, ＿＿＿＿＿＿＿＿＿＿＿＿＿＿＿＿＿＿＿＿＿＿＿＿＿＿＿

Task for Output 2

Model Paragraph 2　　　　　　　　　　　　　 DL 05　CD05

　People claim that fast food is a primary cause of obesity and diabetes. They contain a lot of sugar, salt, and fat. Such ingredients are substantially used to create strong and tempting flavors which people easily become addicted to. If you eat fast food too frequently, there is a chance of getting health  problems. In the U.S., some people sued a big hamburger chain because they gained too much weight after eating the high calorie food on a daily basis. This may be an extraordinary case, but you need to think about the risks for small children. They tend to become junk food addicts innocently and unconsciously. To avoid such problems, some primary schools have started programs to teach proper eating habits.

Model Paragraph 2 で述べられている内容について、自分の意見を英語で3〜4文で書きなさい。理由や、その裏付けとなる具体例も書きなさい。▶ **Template 2** [p. 13]

_____

_____

_____

_____

■ *Self-editing*

1. 結束ができているか確認しなさい。

2. 基本パラグラフの Move が構築されているか確認しなさい。

■ *Peer Review:* Make some comments.

それぞれの意見を読んで、お互いにコメントを書きなさい。

_____

_____

_____

_____

Task for Output 3

Model Paragraph 3, 4 を読み、食の安全に関する問題について自分の意見を述べなさい。

Model Paragraph 3

 DL 06　CD06

Is Your Chicken Safe?

Nowadays there are many food recall cases in individual countries. Last month one of the major fast-food hamburger chains was forced to pull chicken nuggets from 2,000 restaurants. The nuggets were infected with some kind of bacteria. More than 100 customers were sent to hospital. According to the  company, they import chicken products from a factory in China. Sanitary conditions were found to be very bad.

■ *Group Work:* Talk with your classmates about food safety, such as food poisoning, food recall and modified gene products. Refer to the following news.

Model Paragraph 4

New Technology Might Solve Famine

Because of rapid population growth, many countries face difficulty ensuring food supplies. People even lack sufficient food to lead a normal life. Several multinational food companies insist that we should introduce genetically modified (GM) seeds. Such seeds produce large amounts of products compared with natural ones. Big supermarkets have actually already sold vegetables grown with GM seeds. However, some scientists claim that they could have risks to human health.

Model Paragraph 3, 4 に関して、次の 1 ～ 4 に答えなさい。

1. Based on what you learned in the above two paragraphs, what is your opinion about current food safety issues?

_____

_____

2. Why do you think so?

_____

_____

3. Do you have any examples or evidence?

_____

_____

4. Now put them together and develop a short paragraph. ▶ **Template 2** [p. 13]

_____

_____

_____

_____

■ *Self-editing*

1. 結束ができているか確認しなさい。

2. 基本パラグラフの Move が構築されているか確認しなさい。

■ *Peer Review:* Make some comments.

1. パラグラフの Move と英文の結束をお互いに確認しなさい。

2. それぞれの意見を読んで、お互いにコメントを書きなさい。

_____

_____

_____

_____

Task for Output 4

食の安全のためにはどのような活動が必要か、その理由も含めて英語で述べなさい。

_____

_____

_____

_____

_____

_____

_____

句読点 2

■ コロン［:］
コロンは that is「つまりそれは」という意味を持ち、その前にある情報の説明や該当する物の例示をする時に使います。

1. リストの前のコロン
例 It can be said that our life is divided into three equal parts: 8 hours of sleep, 8 hours of work, 8 hours of recreation.

2. 前の情報の説明や定義
例 The pace of our life speeds up: we move faster from one place to another, ...

■ セミコロン［;］
セミコロンは後ろにコメントの追加をしたり、理由を説明したりする時に使います。

1. 接続詞の代わりに使う
例 Ordering too much food can lead to eating too much; it is vital to control yourself.

2. 接続詞とともに使い、節を並べる
例 Parents may be important teachers for children; however, they are not always the best teachers.

・コンマ、セミコロン、ピリオドの順で区切りが強くなります。

Quiz │ 次の英文に適切な句読点を入れ、書き直しなさい。

1. Tom plays many musical instruments piano guitar and violin.

_____

2. She went to the restaurant she ate pasta.

_____

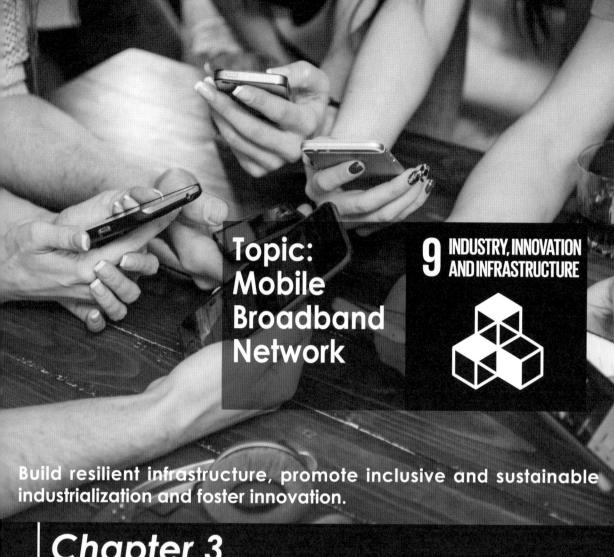

Topic:
Mobile
Broadband
Network

9 INDUSTRY, INNOVATION AND INFRASTRUCTURE

Build resilient infrastructure, promote inclusive and sustainable industrialization and foster innovation.

Chapter 3
Developing Coherence

■ **Pre-Task :** Talk with your classmates about good points and bad points of mobile phones.

☑ **Strategic Points** ⋯ Grammatical cohesion
　　　　　　　　　　　 Vocabulary cohesion
　　　　　　　　　　　 Creating variety of vocabulary

　This chapter focuses on how to develop coherence for reader-centered approaches. In particular, you will learn strategies for cohesion.

▶ この章で学ぶこと ▶ パラグラフの一貫性の構築
　　　　　　　　　 ▶ 文法的結束と語彙的結束の作り方

Strategic Focus 3: Developing Coherence

読みやすい英文を書くための一貫性（coherence）を構築するには、topic sentence を中心にパラグラフ内の文が結束されている必要があります。結束には<u>文法的結束（grammatical cohesion）</u>と<u>語彙的結束（vocabulary cohesion）</u>があります。

Task 1

次の英文はどのように結束していますか。

The mobile phone has become an integral part of our daily lives. iPhone has played the role of an assistant in everyone's life since its introduction.

▶ **Clue**　どのようにして既知情報を作っているか確認する。

Writing Strategy 8　Grammatical Cohesion

文法的な規則に則って語彙を関連させて結束を作る際は、以下のような語句を使います。前方の文に記述されたことを既知情報として言い換える時に使います。

・定冠詞	a firm → the firm	・指示代名詞	物事 → this, that, these, those
・人称代名詞	人名 → he, she, they	・比較語	same, such, so, some, others

Task 2

次のパラグラフで結束を作っている語彙を○で囲み、どこと結びついているか示しなさい。

Model Paragraph 1

 DL 08　CD08

Having equal access to new technology such as IT is important for sustainable development. It enables people to improve their daily lives by getting critical information and helping each other. One such technology, mobile phones, has a lot of advantages for developing countries. In these areas, signal coverage has improved a great deal and now more than 90 percent of people live in covered areas. Regarding this trend, some people say only good things. Yet others point out some negative effects of overuse.

■ *Group Work:* Check the answers with your classmates.

グループになって Task 2 の答えを確認しなさい。

Task 3

次の英文を文法的結束を使って書き換えなさい。

1. Mobile phones have a wide array of uses. Mobile phones benefit users in many ways.

_____

_____

2. iPhone was invented by Steve Jobs. Jobs successfully involved many vendors to develop cutting edge technologies.

_____

_____

3. A mobile phone can be used as a compass for navigating people. A compass for navigating people is very helpful when visiting new places.

_____

_____

Task for Output 1

Group Work: Talk about the benefits of using mobile phones and write them down.

_____

_____

_____

Write It Down: Raise the benefits of using mobile phones. Write your opinions of them.

Template 3 ■ Describing Opinions or Ideas in Order	
議論の観点を示す	There are three advantages ...
1つ目の観点	First, ...
2つ目の観点	Second, ...
3つ目の観点	Third / Finally, ...

_____

_____

_____

_____

Finally, _____

■ *Self-editing*

各文が既知から新規の流れになっているか、確認しなさい。

Writing Strategy *9* Vocabulary Cohesion

語彙的結束とは、同じ意味を持つ異なる形式の語彙を使うことで、文同士を結束させることです。

- ・ 派生語　　manage → manager, management
- ・ 類義語　　company → corporation
- ・ 上位語　　convenience store → retailer
- ・ 下位語　　the car industry → Toyota
- ・ 一般名詞 → thing

─Task 4

次のパラグラフで結束を作っている語彙を○で囲み、どこと結びついているか示しなさい。

Model Paragraph 2　　　　　　　 DL 09　 CD09

Scientists reveal critical findings about negative effects caused by spending too much time on mobile phones. Overuse of mobile phones can be linked to anxiety and severe depression in teens. Young students constantly check their Instagram, LINE or Facebook account. Such social network services
never let them go. Some scientific data clearly indicate a link between the rise of smartphone usage and growing rates of depression and suicide attempts. Addictions to social networks could cause mental illness.

■ *Group Work:* Check the answers with your classmates.

グループになって Task 4 の答えを確認しなさい。

Task 5

次の英文を語彙的結束を使って書き換えなさい。

1. A new study has linked anxiety to the growing use of Facebook and Instagram. The growing use of Facebook and Instagram leads to severe depression as well.

_____

_____

_____

2. GPS technology of mobile phones enables you to find the place you want to go. The place you want to go is shown on the screen. Moreover, you can find out how to go there. The easiest way to get there is also suggested by the application.

_____

_____

_____

_____

Task for Output 2

■ **Group Work:** Talk about negative issues of using mobile phones and write them down.

_____

_____

_____

■ **Write It Down:** Write your opinion about the disadvantages of using mobile phones. Raise three points. ▶ **Template 3** [p. 21]

I think there are three negative points _____

_____

_____

_____

_____

■ Self-editing

各文が既知から新規の流れになっているか確認しなさい。

Writing Strategy **10** Describing Good Points and Bad Points

次のようなテンプレートを使うと、事象の良い点と悪い点を並列して述べて、客観的な議論をすることができます。

Template 4 ■ Describing Advantages and Disadvantages	
利点・欠点の認識	・There are advantages and disadvantages ... ・... have advantages as well as disadvantages
利点を述べる 利点 1 利点 2 利点 3	I'll start from the advantages ...
欠点を述べる 欠点 1 欠点 2 欠点 3	On the other hand, there are several disadvantages ...
結論	After thinking about advantages and disadvantages ...

▶ **Attention!**　benefits and losses や positive and negative も利点や欠点の表現となる。

Task for Output 3

Template 4 を活用して、自分で書いた Task for Output 1 と 2 をまとめ、Mobile phone の良い点と悪い点についてノートに英文で書きなさい。

Task for Output 4

Model Paragraph 3

 DL 10 CD10

Connect or Disconnect?

Although the internet provides a lot of benefits for our modern life, it has changed our life in terms of real interaction with our family and friends. By using SNS, we can keep in touch with many friends and meet new people online. However, a correlation between SNS use and the decline in social relationships has been found. Young people have easily become addicted to life on the mobile screen. They tend to withdraw from personal contact and social involvement, such as sitting together with others and talking about their real feelings. It can be said that they live in a virtual world with virtual friends.

Model Paragraph 3 を読んで自分の意見を書きなさい。 ▶ **Template I** [p. 7]

I agree / disagree _____

_____

_____

_____

_____

_____

_____

_____

Task 6

次ページの Focus on Accuracy を参考にして、Task for Output 3 と 4 で書いたパラグラフの限定詞を○で囲みなさい。

限定詞と冠詞その1

■ 限定詞［this, those / my, their / another, all, many / 冠詞］

　名詞句の前には、必ず冠詞などの限定詞をつけます。

　名詞句とは、名詞を中心にした句としてのまとまりです。例えば the reliable food は、定冠詞の the と修飾語の形容詞 reliable が名詞の food の前について、一つの名詞句を形成しています。名詞は、それがどのような性質を表すのか、読者に<u>情報を特定化して限定する必要があります</u>。その際に使われるのが「限定詞（determiner）」と呼ばれるもので、<u>必ず名詞句の前につけます</u>。

　イメージ：〔　限定詞　〕　名詞句

　限定詞には主に、this や those などの指示詞、my や their などの所有限定詞、another, all, many などの数量詞、そして冠詞が使われます。
- 指示詞　　　　　this service「このサービス」
- 所有限定詞　　　our service「我々のサービス」
- 数量詞　　　　　another service「別のサービス」
- 冠詞　　　　　　a/the service「ある／特定のサービス」

■ 冠詞［a, the, Ø］

　限定詞の位置に入る冠詞は a, the, Ø（ゼロ冠詞／無冠詞：つまり何も入らない）の3種類です。Øのゼロ冠詞とは、限定詞の位置に a や the がない状態です。この考え方に慣れると日本人もエラーが減ります。例えば、plan という名詞には以下の3つのタイプの冠詞を選択することができます。

1. a plan　　　：〔　a　〕plan　　　　「いわゆる1つの計画」
2. the plan(s)：〔　the　〕plan(s)　　「特定の1つ（または複数の）計画」
3. plans　　　：〔　Ø　〕plans　　　「一般的な複数ある計画」

　1のように、冠詞の a は名詞の単数形の前にしか入りません。the は2のように、名詞の単数形・複数形どちらの前にも入ることができます。また、3のように名詞の複数形の前には Ø が入る（冠詞が何も入らない）ことが多くなります。

　Quiz│ 次の英文の空所に何を入れたらよいか考えなさい。

　I saw (　　　) cat. It was very cute.

　cat は可算名詞の単数形なので Ø は入りません。この文だけでは、a も the も入る可能性があります。不定冠詞 a が入ると、書き手は「かわいい猫」と不特定多数の猫のうちの1匹を意味していることになります。一方、the の場合は、書き手と読者は「共に特定の猫を知っている」という前提で情報を伝えています。

Writing Tip by Corpus Analysis 1
—語彙的結束を活用して語彙の多様性を構築

　英文エッセイの評価では、「多様な語彙を使用しているか」が必須項目になります。これを実現するためには、語彙的結束を活用しパラグラフ内の語彙を言い換えます。

　次のリストは、コーパス分析で明らかになった英文エッセイに特徴的に多く使用される語彙と、それらの語彙的結束が可能な特徴語です。書き換えができるようになりましょう。

語彙グループ	代表的な特徴語	語彙的結束によって書き換えられる特徴語
利点・長所	advantage(s)	benefit(s), beneficial, good point(s)
欠点・問題	disadvantage(s)	trouble(s), problem(s), mistake(s)
重要さ	important	essential
成功・達成	success	succeed, achieve
機会	opportunity(ies)	chance(s)
仕事・課題	work	job(s), task(s)
人	people	person, human, humankind
生活	life	living
助け・協力	help	support, teamwork
学生・若者	student(s)	teenager(s), young
友人・仲間	friend(s)	classmate(s), roommate(s), friendship
学び・教育	learn	learning, study, knowledge, lesson(s), education
教え	teach	teacher, teaching, supervisor, educator
旅行・移動	travel	trip, transportation, movement
好む	prefer	preference, favorite

**Topic:
AI and
Singularity**

**9 INDUSTRY, INNOVATION
AND INFRASTRUCTURE**

Build resilient infrastructure, promote inclusive and sustainable
industrialization and foster innovation.

Chapter 4
Guiding Your Readers

Pre-Task : Talk with your classmates about future technology: AI.

Strategic Points ⋯Raising awareness of readers
                        Use of metadiscourse

You will learn how to guide readers to follow your points. In particular, the
focus is on the relevant use of metadiscourse for persuasive writing.

この章で学ぶこと ▶ 読者の誘導の仕方
　　　　　　　　 ▶ 効果的なメタディスコースの使い方

Strategic Focus 4: Guiding Readers by Metadiscourse

読者を上手に誘導することで、書いてある内容を把握させ、理解しやすくする必要があります。そのためのシグナルとして文頭のメタディスコースを使います。通常、文頭は既知情報から始まります。その位置にメタディスコースを置くと文の流れが途切れ、読者の注意を喚起します。そこに後に続く文の読み方を示すと読みやすくなるのです。

Task 1

次の英文はどのようにすると読みやすくなりますか。

An AI revolution can happen, and the outcome could be very good for our society. It doesn't happen automatically.

▶ **Clue** 2つの文に一貫性はあるか？

Writing Strategy 11 Use of Metadiscourse

文頭の既知情報の前に置くメタディスコースは、以下の3つに分類できます。

1. 接合表現：接続詞、接続副詞など。一般にはディスコースマーカーとも呼ばれる。
   Therefore, However, For example, First
2. 筆者の態度・コメント：後続の情報への考えや判断の示唆。書き手の立場：スタンス（stance）
   In my opinion, It is widely assumed
3. 注意の喚起：読者への直接の働きかけ
   As you can see, Consider now

Task 2

次のパラグラフのメタディスコースを抜き出し、それぞれの役割を述べなさい。

Model Paragraph 1

 DL 11 CD11

Science fiction describes artificial intelligence (AI) as robots with human-like characteristics. For example, these robots can consider complex contexts and provide the most relevant solution. In the last decades, people doubted such things would happen soon. However, AI has been progressing much faster 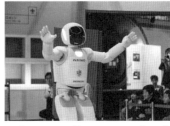 than expected. Now it outperforms humans in playing chess or Japanese shogi. Moreover, we can enjoy many AI products, from Amazon Alexa to self-driving cars.

· _____ 役割：_____
· _____ 役割：_____
· _____ 役割：_____
· _____ 役割：_____

Task for Output 1

■ **Group Work:** Talk about other AI services and products and their benefits, and write them down.

_____

_____

■ **Write It Down:** Write about your favorite AI products or services. How have they changed your life? Can you think of any new useful products or services?

Recent AI technologies are very _____

_____

First, _____

_____

Second, _____

_____

In the near future I would like to have _____

_____

This is because _____

_____

■ **Self-editing**

すべての名詞の限定詞を確認しなさい。

■ **Peer Review:** Make some comments.

それぞれの意見を読んで、お互いにコメントを書きなさい。

_____

_____

Writing Strategy **12** Use of Discourse Marker

接合表現：文頭の接続詞や接続副詞でよく使われるものに以下のメタディスコースがあります。

1. 反意的

例　Some people think AI will control our lives. However, others claim that it is science fiction.

2. 付加的

例　Autonomous weapons equipped with AI could easily cause mass casualties. Moreover, an AI arms race might lead to an AI war.

3. 例示

例　New applications solve problems with great efficiency. For example, they can find the most relevant URL as a source of reference.

4. 時間的

例　There are three steps for registering on this website. First, you need to provide your address.

5. 因果的

例　Many online services are becoming cheaper. Therefore, it has become easier for ordinary people to use them.

6. 結論

例　In conclusion, children find it hard to put down their mobile phones and they become addicted to SNS.

━*Task 3*━

次の英文の空所1〜4に、もっとも適切なメタディスコースを選択肢から選び書き入れなさい。

People discuss whether AI is something we should fear or welcome. Many recognize its efficiency in finding a solution for certain problems. (¹·　　　　　), some claim that it could have several negative impacts on our lives. (²·　　　　　), people are concerned about their job security. (³·　　　　　), many jobs will be performed better by machines than human beings. (⁴·　　　　　), workers who deal with routine tasks may lose their income source. To improve the situation, we need to introduce human resource training focused on developing skills involving human interaction.

For example	First	Consequently	However

Task for Output 2

■ **Group Work:** Talk with your classmates about the following questions.

1. What kind of jobs can be replaced by AI?
2. What kind of jobs done by humans will we still need in the future?

■ **Write It Down:** Write your opinion about future job situations.

以下のテンプレートを活用して、ノートに英文で自分の考えをまとめなさい。

Template 5 ■ Adding Reasons for Advantages and Disadvantages	
導入文	例 AI may significantly change job contexts.
良い点	I'll start from advantages ...
理由／例	This is because ... / For example ...
悪い点	On the other hand, there are several disadvantages ...
理由／例	This is because ... / For example ...
まとめ	例 Although AI can solve ...

■ **Self-editing**

1. 結束ができているか確認しなさい。
2. 適切にメタディスコースが使われているか確認しなさい。

■ **Peer Review:** Make some comments.

それぞれの英文を読んで、お互いに短いコメントを書きなさい。

Writing Strategy *13* Describing Your Stance

スタンスを表すメタディスコースには以下のようなものがあります。

1. 自分の意見や考えを述べる
   I think, I believe, I would like to say, I am sure that
   In my opinion, As far as I am concerned
2. 予期しない結果や否定的内容の提示　Unfortunately
3. 特記すべきこと、興味深い発見や報告の示唆
   Interestingly, Remarkably, Surprisingly
4. 話題の特定化や一般化　In particular, In general
5. 類似性や代替性　Similarly, Alternatively

Task 4

Model Paragraph 2と3の文頭のメタディスコースに下線を引き、それぞれの役割を答えなさい。

Model Paragraph 2

I wonder what would happen in a world dominated by AI based on big personal data. I am sure that people need massive data to develop more sophisticated AI systems. Surprisingly, IT companies are gradually collecting our personal information by storing cookies on our mobiles and PCs through our web browser. I do not like the idea that someone is stealing my personal data to expand their business. Whenever I browse web pages, some companies' advertisements pop up to urge me to visit their shopping sites.

Model Paragraph 3

Do you think AI can save your life by collecting your personal data? I used to think that someone would only buy a wearable watch to show off. However, these watches have incredible functions that can save lives. An old man was given an Apple Watch as a birthday present by his daughter. She thought the watch could monitor his health condition. One night the watch woke him up. It told him that his resting heart rate was elevated while sleeping and that he should see a doctor. Although he did not feel sick, signs of a heart attack were discovered. Since then he never takes off his watch.

Task for Output 3

After reading Model Paragraphs 2 and 3, describe good points and bad points of heavy dependence on AI.

AI に依存することの利点と問題点について、ノートに英文で意見を書きなさい。

▶ **Template 4** [p. 24]

■ *Self-editing*

1. 結束ができているか確認しなさい。
2. 適切にメタディスコースが使われているか確認しなさい。

■ *Peer Review:* Check the coherence and make some comments.

1. ペアの英文に結束ができているか確認しなさい。
2. ペアの英文に適切にメタディスコースが使われているか確認しなさい。
3. それぞれの英文を読んで、お互いにコメントを書きなさい。

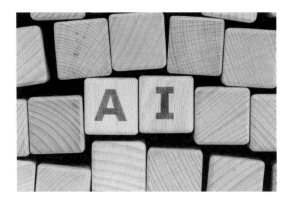

限定詞と冠詞その２

■名詞と冠詞

冠詞は、その後に来る名詞の種類によって使い方が決まります。冠詞を決定する一般名詞の可算・不可算名詞の確認が必要です。

1. 可算名詞：概念的に数えることができ、通常は単数と複数で形を変えます。
- 単数：冠詞は a か the　　複数：冠詞は the か∅（何も入らない）
- es/s など複数を示す接尾語をつける
- people や police など集合名詞は複数を示す接尾語をつけない

2. 不可算名詞：概念的に単数複数の区別がなく、冠詞は ∅ か the になります。
- 抽象名詞：目に見えない概念　例 work（労働）、happiness（幸福）
- 物質名詞：目に見えるが区切ることが難しいもの　例 milk（牛乳）

Quiz 次の英文のそれぞれの名詞と冠詞を確認しなさい。

1. Some people spend money on luxury brands.
2. Some people spend money on a luxury brand.
3. Some people spend money on the luxury brands.

名詞は people, money, brand(s) の３つあり、それぞれの冠詞を確認する必要があります。以下が１〜３の構造で、〔　〕は冠詞の位置となります。

1. 〔∅〕Some people spend 〔∅〕money on 〔∅〕luxury brands.
2. 〔∅〕Some people spend 〔∅〕money on 〔a〕luxury brand.
3. 〔∅〕Some people spend 〔∅〕money on 〔the〕luxury brands.

▶ **Attention!** 英文の添削で一番エラーが多いのは冠詞の使い方である。
- 最初は面倒だが、すべての名詞を確認する。
- 名詞句には冠詞が必要。英文を書き終えたら、そこに何を入れたのか必ず見直す。
- ゼロ冠詞の可算名詞は複数形を取ることが多く、その形も確認する。

■その他 the が必要な名詞句
- **序数** the first, the second, the last（順番は１つしかない）
- **最上級** the best practice, the most useful item（最上のものは１つ）
- **限定する形容詞** the only, the same（１つの物を限定する）
- **世の中に１つしかない物や団体、出来事** the sea, the sun, the United Nations, the IMF, the Ministry of Education
- **物事の総称となるもの** the rich（富裕層）、the news（ニュース番組）
- **限定する時代や年代** the 1960s, the past four decades

▶ **Attention!** the は読者と共有の情報という合図。「あなたが既に知っている情報ですよ」と伝えることになる。

Writing Tip by Corpus Analysis 2
— エッセイコーパスでよく使われるディスコースマーカー

　Writing Strategy 12（p. 31）で示したもの以外にも英文エッセイに特徴的な文頭のディスコースマーカーがあります。ここでは特に使用頻度の高いものを掲載します。

種類	使用頻度の高い表現	同様の特徴的表現
反意的	However	But, Yet, Nevertheless
対照の導入	While	Instead, On the other hand, In contrast
譲歩	Although	Though, Even though
付加的	Moreover	And, Furthermore, In addition, Besides
例示	For example	For instance
時間・順序	Now Here First Second Finally	Nowadays, Recently Firstly, First of all, At first Then, After that At last
理由	As	Because
因果的	Therefore Consequently	Thus, Accordingly, So As a result
結論・まとめ	In conclusion In summary	To conclude To sum up
代替を示す	Otherwise	

Topic: Ecotourism

14 LIFE BELOW WATER

Conserve and sustainably use the oceans, seas and marine resources for sustainable development.

Chapter 5
Hedges and Boosters

■ **Pre-Task :** Talk with your classmates about your favorite place to travel.

✓ **Strategic Points** ⋯ Hedges
　　　　　　　　　　　 Boosters

　　In order to protect your argument, you need to use hedges which downtone your claims with uncertain expressions such as modals. On the other hand, you can use boosters to highlight your important points and attract readers.

▶ この章で学ぶこと ▶ 議論を弱め、批判に対して防御するヘッジ表現の活用法
　　　　　　　　　　 ▶ 議論を強調するブースター表現の使用法

Strategic Focus 5: Hedges and Boosters

ヘッジ（hedge）表現を使い、読者からの批判に対してあらかじめ防御することで、議論の客観性を向上させます。また、強調すべき内容をブースター（booster）表現で記述すると読者を惹きつけることができ、より説得力のある内容となります。これらも書き手の主張の強さや立場を表すスタンスとなります。（p. 32 の Writing Strategy 13 参照）

Task 1

それぞれの英文の違いはどのような点ですか。

1. Scuba diving is an exciting sport.

2. Scuba diving can be an exciting sport.

3. Scuba diving could be an exciting sport.

Writing Strategy 14 Use of Hedges

ヘッジは主張を抑え丁寧にするだけでなく、議論の防御にも使えます。書き手が断定する度合いを弱めて、読者の批判からの逃げ道を用意します。ヘッジは近似詞（approximator）とシールド（shield）の2種類に分類できます。

1. 近似詞：事象の明確さを弱める

Approximately 10,000 people visit Indonesia to see wild orangutans.

2. シールド：確信の度合いを弱める

Unless we protect them properly, we may lose many endangered species.

Task 2

次のパラグラフのヘッジ表現を抜き出し、それぞれの役割を述べなさい。

Model Paragraph 1

 DL 14　CD14

According to the United Nations World Tourism Organization (UNWTO), the number of tourists internationally could reach approximately 1.4 billion. However, it may not be totally good news. The increase of visitors can lead to significant environmental damage. In order to receive a huge number of travelers, countries need to construct new roads and accommodations by destroying forests and mountains. In many cases, big international companies develop those facilities for their own profit. They might hire some local people, but the local society does not fully enjoy the benefits.

· _____	役割 : _____
· _____	役割 : _____
· _____	役割 : _____
· _____	役割 : _____
· _____	役割 : _____

■ *Group Work:* Check the answers with your classmates.

グループになって Task 2 の答えを確認しなさい。

Task for Output 1

■ *Group Work:* Talk with your classmates about any solutions for Model Paragraph 1.

■ *Write It Down:* Write down your solutions.

以下のテンプレートを活用して、ノートに自分の解決方法をパラグラフでまとめなさい。

Template 6 ■ Writing a Solution

Introductory sentence	I think we should (not) ...
Reasons	This is because ... / In my opinion, ...
Solutions	In order to solve ...
Examples	For example, ...

Writing Strategy 15 Use of Boosters

内容を強調したり、内容の重要さを訴える際にブースター表現を使います。

1. ブースターの役割を持つ動詞

   強い断定の意味を持つ動詞で確信度が高くなり、読み手に強いメッセージを送ることになります。

   confirm, convince, demonstrate, determine, prove

   例 The research <u>proves</u> that ecotourism is critical for protecting nature.

2. ブースターの役割を持つ形容詞、副詞

   以下の形容詞や副詞には、書き手の主張をより明確にする働きがあります。

   clear, definitely, essential, extremely, significant, significantly

   例 It is <u>essential</u> for local people to preserve natural wonders to attract foreign tourists.

3. 文頭のメタディスコース

ブースターの中には、Chapter 4 で示した文頭のメタディスコースにより注意を喚起するものもあります。

Indeed, Of course, It is clear that, No one can deny, It is true

例 No one can deny that tourism is a major source of income in rainforest areas.

Task 3

次のパラグラフからブースター表現を抜き出し、それぞれの意味を確認しなさい。

Model Paragraph 2

 DL 15　CD15

The Philippine economy heavily depends on its natural resources, such as fish. The country is surrounded by incredibly beautiful tropical oceans. Unfortunately, an expanding population and continuing poverty force people to conduct destructive activities, including dynamite fishing.  Although using dynamite to kill many fish at once is illegal, it is the only way for poor locals to make ends meet. David was born in Moalboal on Cebu Island and raised as a fisherman. Since his childhood, he has loved swimming around the magnificent coral reefs. In particular, he has a secret place, Pescador Island, which is off Moalboal coast. It is a paradise for sea animals. He wanted to preserve the nature there, but couldn't stop others from using dynamite.

· _____　意味：_____
· _____　意味：_____
· _____　意味：_____
· _____　意味：_____

■ **Group Work:** Check the answers with your classmates.

グループになって Task 3 の答えを確認しなさい。

Task for Output 2

What do you think about the story in Model Paragraph 2? Can you think of any solutions?

前のページの Template 6 を使って、ノートに英文で解決方法を書きなさい。

■ *Self-editing*

1. 結束ができているか確認しなさい。

2. 適切にヘッジやブースターが使われているか確認しなさい。

■ *Peer Review:* Make some comments.

1. ペアの英文の Self-editing を確認しなさい。

2. ペアの英文を読んで、短いコメントを書きなさい。

Task for Output 3

Would you like to try scuba diving?

Model Paragraph 3

 DL 16 CD16

   One day a Dutch scuba diver visited David's village and asked David to take him to Pescador Island in his fishing boat. David took the diver to one of the most beautiful coral areas. After one hour, the diver came up to the boat and said, "This is a miracle! You should check the paradise with your own eyes." The diver stayed for a while and taught David how to begin diving. David saw hundreds of sea animals, such as tuna, sardines, snappers, barracudas, Napoleon fish, sawfish, sharks, turtles, and whale sharks against the colorful reefs. The underwater area of this small island has a unique shape, with tunnels, caverns and steep drop-offs, which could attract divers who want to see a variety of marine life. David decided to open a scuba diving shop to share these gifts from nature with other divers. He started with three sets of secondhand diving equipment and six scuba tanks. Gradually, rumors of the incredible diving in Pescador spread by word of mouth, and many divers came to see it.

■ *Group Work:* Ask the following questions to your classmates.

1. Do you like marine sports? Why or why not?

2. What kind of images do you have of scuba diving?

3. Would you like to try it? Why or why not?

■ *Write It Down:* Write your opinion about marine sports such as scuba diving.

▶ **Template 2** [p. 13]

_____

_____

_____

_____

■ *Self-editing*

1. 結束ができているか確認しなさい。

2. 限定詞が適切に使われているか確認しなさい。

Task for Output 4

What do you think about ecotourism?

Model Paragraph 4

 DL 17 CD17

The more divers came to Pescador, the more jobs were created around Moalboal village. Western visitors needed local restaurants, bars, and accommodations. Their spending money for scuba diving and other activities for one day was equivalent to the average monthly income of local people. David insisted that villagers stop dynamite fishing, which destroyed their precious natural resources attracting many foreign travelers. He advised them to change their jobs to operating boats for diving, providing local transportation, or opening seafood restaurants for visitors. Gradually his campaign started working and everybody took action to protect the natural beauty. In his scuba training, visitors learned how to deal with fragile coral reefs and protect the sea world. After participating in David's diving course, visitors gained not only a scuba license, but also knowledge about how to live with precious nature. David became a leader for enhancing, protecting and enjoying nature in the area, and was elected as a local governor. Now he is very busy educating people about the value of ecotourism. He also plays the role of chairman of the Committee on Tourism that supports environmental protection and conservation of the Philippines.

■ *Group Work:* Talk about ecotourism with your classmates.

1. What are essential elements of ecotourism?

2. Why do we need ecotourism?

3. Do you know about any other example of ecotourism?

■ *Write It Down*

Model Paragraph 4 を参照し、次のテンプレートを参考にして、ノートにエコツーリズムについて英語で自分の意見をまとめなさい。

Template 7 ■ Writing Your Opinion	
Introductory sentence General statement	例 Ecotourism should be spread ...
Reasons	
Examples or explanations	例 For instance, David attempted to improve peoples' lives and maintain natural wonders in Cebu by expanding his scuba diving business.
Conclusion	In conclusion, I believe ...

■ *Self-editing*

1. 結束ができているか確認しなさい。

2. 適切にヘッジやブースターが使われているか確認しなさい。

■ *Peer Review:* Make some comments.

1. ペアの英文の Self-editing を確認しなさい。

2. ペアの英文を読んで、短いコメントを書きなさい。

_____

_____

_____

Focus on Accuracy : Subject-Verb Agreement

主語と動詞の一致

■ 後に来る情報を限定する後方照応の the

　読者と共有の情報を示す the は、後ろに続く情報を限定する方法があり、これが後方照応の the です。英語エッセイで最もエラーが起きやすい箇所の１つです。

> 例　We admit the **effect** of introducing ecotourism projects is significant.
> 　　　　　　 主要部　　　　　　　　 後方照応

　述部リームにある the effect of introducing ecotourism projects が１つの名詞句です。前置詞 of の前にあるのが、この句の単数や複数の性質を決定する「主要部」となります。of 以下は主要部 effect を、後ろから修飾しています。この場合の限定詞の the は、主要部の後ろに説明があるというシグナルです。このように後に来る情報の意味を限定するため、後方照応と呼ばれます。

■ 名詞句の主要部が後に続く動詞と呼応する

　よくあるエラーに「主語と動詞の一致」の問題があります。これは「主語を、動詞の単数や複数の形と一致させる」という規則によるものです。例えば、主語が単数の場合は、現在形の be 動詞なら is にします。また、主語が３人称で一般動詞なら動詞の末尾に s や es をつけます。名詞句の場合は、その主要部が動詞の単数形や複数形を決めます。

　上の例文をもう一度見てください。be 動詞の形を決めるのはすぐ前にある複数形の名詞 projects ではありません。名詞句の主要部である of の前の effect が単数なので、動詞は呼応して is となります。

Quiz ｜ 次の英文を修正しなさい。

1. The productivity of these environmental tasks were much better than their expectation.

2. The beliefs in the rapid improvement of this project is different from the previous assumption.

▶ *Attention!*
　・主語と動詞が一致しているか常に確認する。
　・長い名詞句が主語の場合は、主要部と動詞を一致させる。

Part 2

Strategies for Paragraph Writing

Part 2 では課題に対する自分の考えを
より具体的に記述する方法を学びます。

Topic: Convenient for Who?

3 GOOD HEALTH AND WELL-BEING

Ensure healthy lives and promote well-being for all at all ages.

Chapter 6
Generating Ideas

■ Pre-Task : Talk with your classmates about your favorite convenience store.

✓ Strategic Points ⋯ Brainstorming   Organizing ideas
Idea listing   Critical thinking
Clustering

You will learn how to generate ideas for essay writing. The focus is on brainstorming techniques including listing, clustering, and organizing ideas.

▶ この章で学ぶこと ▶ 書く内容のアイディアの広げ方とまとめ方
    ▶ 批判的な思考方法

Strategic Focus 6: Brainstorming and Critical Thinking

Brainstorming とは、テーマについて自由にアイディアを出し、概念をまとめ、パラグラフの構成をまとめていく方法です。

Task 1

以下の質問に回答し、クラスメイトにも同じ質問をしなさい。

1. How often do you go to a convenience store?
2. What kinds of goods do you buy at the store?

Writing Strategy 16 Brainstorming

Brainstorming のポイントは、とにかく思いつくままに、できるだけ多くの単語を書き出すことです。10 分程度で思いつくことを書き留めます。最初は日本語でも構いませんが、慣れてきたらできるだけ英語で書きましょう。

▶ *Attention!*

・Brainstorming は書き出すアイディアの数が重要
・あまり深く考えず、頭に浮かんだことをどんどん書き出す

Task 2

「コンビニ」と聞いて、思いつく単語をできるだけたくさん書き、リストにしなさい。この時点では英語でも日本語でも構いません。

Group Work: Check the answers with your classmates.

クラスメイトと書き出した単語を比較し、日本語の単語は英語に書き換えなさい。

Task 3

次のページのパラグラフを読んで自分のリストと比較しなさい。また、後の質問に対する答えを書きなさい。

The Role of Convenience Stores

There are more than 56,000 convenience stores in Japan and the number is still increasing. Nowadays, they are an important part of our life and it is difficult to imagine life without them. They are almost everywhere in this country and sell everything from rice balls to cigarettes 24 hours a day. You can buy a variety of food, desserts, and drinks including alcohol. You can even get stationery, underwear, and special envelopes for funerals. Most of the convenience stores offer services like bill paying, tickets for entertainment, photograph printing, copy machines, and ATMs. They can be a landmark to find your destination on the road and a place to stop for a bathroom. More interestingly, as they are still brightly lit at midnight, they can become safe places for people in need of help, such as potential victims of stalkers and other criminals. In the case of natural disasters, such as a big earthquake, some convenience stores can be a base for the delivery of emergency supplies including water.

1. Why do you think the number of convenience stores is increasing?

_____

2. Who is the convenience store competitor and why?

_____

Writing Strategy 17 Clustering

Brainstorming で抽出した単語を、似たようなものでグループ分けし cluster map を作ります。ここでは、中心の main topic に convenience store を書き入れます。続いて、グループ分けしたクラスターの subtopic を結びつけます。そこからさらに、そのキーワードに関連する語をつなげていきます。

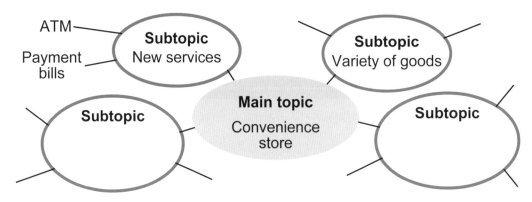

Task 4

前のページの cluster map を参考に、自分の brainstorming による cluster map をノートに完成させなさい。

Writing Strategy 18 Listing

Listing は、作成した cluster map の中から、特に興味のある、または書きやすい subtopic を３つ選んで作ります。それぞれをパラグラフのリストとして並べます。この際 Template 8 の Outlining を利用して書く内容をまとめていきます。

Template 8 ■ Outlining

Topic sentence	*In modern society we cannot live without convenience stores.*
Supporting sentence 1	Subtopic: *convenient for shopping* Example: *variety of goods*
Supporting sentence 2	Subtopic: *useful services* Example: *ATM*
Supporting sentence 3	Subtopic: *as a landmark* Example: *to find a location*
Concluding sentence	*In summary, convenience stores are essential for our daily life.*

1. はじめに topic sentence のポイントを書きます。
2. subtopic のキーワードを書きます。
3. キーワードをより具体的に説明する例を書きます。
4. 最後にまとめとなるポイントを書きます。

Task for Output 1

Complete your outline of the convenience stores and its competitors.

コンビニとその競争相手に関する cluster map をノートに作り、Outline を完成させなさい。

Topic sentence	
Convenience stores	Subtopic: 例 Increase of convenience stores Reasons:
Competitors 1	Subtopic: 例 Discounters Reasons:
Competitors 2	Subtopic: 例 Online shopping Reasons:
Concluding sentence	

■ Write It Down

Convenience Stores and Competitors というタイトルでノートに英文を完成させましょう。

Writing Strategy 19 Critical Thinking

Critical Thinking（CT）とは、事象を批判的に捉え、自分のオリジナルな考えを産出する方法です。次のような観点で、一般に言われていることや、誰かの主張の根拠を調べ、客観性があるのか確認します。

1. What is the purpose of the argument?
   書いている議論の目的は何か、それは適切か。
2. Why does the author want to make this claim?
   なぜそれを主張しているのか、それは妥当か。
3. How does the author persuade readers of his points?
   どの方法で説得を試みているのか、それは適切か。
4. What is the evidence? その根拠は何か、それは妥当か。
5. Is there any counterevidence? 反証する証拠はないか。

Input for Writing 1 に対する CT の例を以下に挙げます。

1. 目的：コンビニは便利なので数が増えている。
   CT コンビニ店舗が増えると、これまでの住環境にどのような変化をもたらすか。
2. 理由：コンビニは我々の生活になくてはならない。
   CT これまではどのようにしていたのか。
3. 方法：消費者に様々な新しい価値を提供している。
   CT それらはすべて良い影響ばかりか。

4. いくつかの具体的な商品やサービス

    CT そのようなサービスを提供するために働く人や周りの環境はどう変わったか。

5. コンビニができたことによるデメリット

    CT 周りの住民や地域、社会に与える悪影響は何か。

■ *Group Work:* Input for Writing 1 に対して例として挙げられた CT について、あなたの考えをクラスメイトと話し合いなさい。

Task for Output 2

Write your opinions about good things and bad things about convenience stores.

Input for Writing 2

 DL 19 CD19

Not Always Convenient

Although convenience stores seem to be essential for our lifestyle, we need to bear in mind their negative aspects. They may have harmful effects on local communities and environmental issues. As convenience stores are open even in the middle of the night, they could attract consumers with bad behavior who fool around riding motorbikes and cars that make a lot of noise. They sometimes throw their garbage anywhere around the stores. Local people may be threatened by shoplifters or street gangs. Regarding environmental problems, convenience stores use a great amount of energy. They are open 24 hours and waste a lot of electricity with bright lights, air-conditioners, and huge refrigerators. On top of that, they produce an enormous amount of garbage, including leftover foods and drinks. They are so strict about the image of freshness that they throw away much food that can still be consumed.

■ *Generating Ideas:* Write your answers to the following questions.

1. What do you think about the above issue?

_____

_____

2. Why do you think so?

_____

_____

3. What are examples?

_____

_____

■ *Making a Cluster Map:* Write about the positive and negative effects of the increasing number of convenience stores.

左に良い点、右に悪い点を記入して cluster map を完成させなさい。

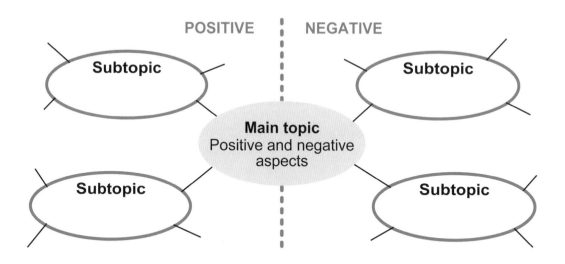

■ *Completing Your Outline*

Cluster map を活用して以下のテンプレートにキーワードを記入し、outline を完成させなさい。

Topic sentence	Convenience stores have both positive and negative effects on our society.
Positive	Subtopic 1: Example: Subtopic 2: Example:
Negative	Subtopic 1: Example: Subtopic 2: Example:
Concluding sentence	

■ *Write It Down:* Write your opinion about convenience stores.

ノートに英文で自分の意見をまとめなさい。

Focus on Accuracy : Hedges

ヘッジに使われる法助動詞

■can, could による可能性・確信度のヘッジ

can は、可能性に「事実や経験に基づく客観性がある」時に用いられます。一般に could は「理論上は可能な（theoretically possible）」ことを表し、「理論的にはありえるかもしれないが、実際はそれほど可能性があることではない」というシグナルを送ります。can から could へと次第に書き手の確信度は低くなります。例 1 では、コンビニの重要性を結論づけていますが、can を使うことで「可能性」としての主張を少し弱めています。例 2 では、あくまで理論的にはそのように言えるが、例外もあることを示唆しています。

例 1　We **can** conclude that convenience stores are important for our life.

例 2　We **could** conclude that convenience stores are important for our life.

■may, might による可能性・確信度のヘッジ

may は主観的な判断に基づき述べる場合に使われます。事実や経験に基づく客観性は弱いので、can に比べると確信度は低いと言えます。重大な内容で、根拠がそれほど強くない時などに用いられます。また might は、さらに可能性の低い状況で使われます。「とても稀なケースとして、ないわけではない」というニュアンスとなります。書き手の主張としては確信度が低く、曖昧な表現です。例 3 のように may を使うと、「女性が（社会での地位や階層の）移動を妨げるような障害に出会う可能性はそれほど大きくない」という書き手のスタンスを示します。また、例 4 のように might では、かなりまれで、あまり起きない事象として考えていることが示唆されます。

例 3　Female workers **may** encounter barriers to upward mobility.

例 4　Female workers **might** encounter barriers to upward mobility.

Quiz ｜ 次の各文の違いを考えなさい。

1. It is said that convenience stores have negative aspects.
2. It can be said that convenience stores have negative aspects.
3. It could be said that convenience stores have negative aspects.

Topic:
Fair Trade

1 NO POVERTY

End poverty in all its forms everywhere.

Chapter 7
How to Attract Your Readers

■ **Pre-Task :** Talk with your classmates about imported food products from developing countries.

☑ **Strategic Points** ⋯ Attracting audience
　　　　　　　　　　　Topic and controlling ideas

　　In this chapter, you will learn how to attract your readers at the very beginning of your paragraph. We focus on how to develop your topic sentence.

▶ この章で学ぶこと ▶ 読者を惹きつけるための topic sentence の書き方

Strategic Focus 7: Developing Effective Topic Sentence

読者が読みたくなるような、わかりやすいパラグラフを構築するために topic sentence を効果的に書く必要があります。

━Task 1━

次の英文の後にどのような内容が続くか、クラスメイトと話し合い、思いつく英文を書きなさい。

Millions of people who live on farms in developing countries cannot earn enough to support their families for several reasons.

_____

_____

Writing Strategy 20 How to Start Your Paragraph Effectively

効果的なパラグラフの書き出し

パラグラフを書く時は、最初に読者に十分興味を持たせる工夫が必要です。内容を示唆して読むべき価値があることを訴えます。この際、読みやすくしたり読者の注意を引いたりするために、以下の5つの導入文（introductory sentence）のパターンがよく活用されます。

1. 一般的な事象の把握から始める

   例 Great changes have taken place in family life in modern society.

2. 多くの権威者や研究者が重要な話題と認識していることを示す

   例 According to many psychology researchers, people keep themselves involved in hard work to preserve their positions.

3. 興味深い逸話から始める

   例 With the growing use of computers both in the classroom and at home, the level of literacy of students is dropping.

4. 歴史的な背景を述べる

   例 The ancient cities of South America were designed with large public buildings to show the dignity of the kingdoms.

5. 統計などの数字を使い、議論する課題の重要性や普遍性を訴える

   例 Survey results show that 70% of parents think that Japanese television programs are connected to their children's poor behavior in public.

Task 2

次の導入文は、それぞれ5つの導入文（introductory sentence）のパターンのどれに該当するか、番号を記入しなさい。

a. The fair trade movement is widespread in England, where there are 90 universities, and over 3,000 schools registered in the Fairtrade Education Scheme. [   ]

b. The history of British trade in their colonies left negative assets to African countries. [   ]

c. By 2050, Africa will become the most populous region of the world. [   ]

d. Many researchers point out that the world organization should take immediate actions to help poor farmers in developing countries. [   ]

e. Recently people have recognized the importance of Fairtrade campaigns.

[   ]

Task for Output 1

Describe your opinion about developing countries' problems.

Input for Writing 1

 DL 20   CD20

Background

European colonialism since the 17th century has led to economic inequality in the world today. Empires such as England, France and Spain conquered many areas in Asia, Africa, and the Americas for their own economic benefit. They sometimes destroyed social infrastructures and local people's lifestyles by expanding their territories for colonies. Industrial groups from Europe became dictators forcing invaded lands to produce raw material goods or crops. They often exploited natural resources from colonies to achieve economic growth for home countries. These long historical sacrifices discouraged the creation of industry in developing countries even after their independence from colonialism. Indeed, many African countries still struggle from a negative heritage which obstructs economic growth.

■ *Group Work:* Ask your classmates the following questions.

1. What do you think about the above issue?

2. Why do you think so?

3. What can we do to solve the problem?

■ *Write It Down:* Write your opinion about the problems.
ノートに英文で自分の考えをまとめなさい。▶ **Template 7** [p. 43]

■ *Self-editing*

英文に結束ができているか確認しなさい。

Writing Strategy *21* How to Write an Effective Topic Sentence

Chapter 2 で確認したように、topic sentence はパラグラフの話題とその展開の仕方を読者に示します。以下のような、概念を分割できる語彙を話題の展開の部分で使うと効果的です。

前につける修飾語	概念を分割できる語彙	パラグラフで説明する内容
some several many certain different	reasons	理由
	characteristics	特徴
	factors	要因
	differences	違い
	advantages / disadvantages	長所・短所
	good points / bad points	良い点・悪い点
	strengths / weaknesses	強み・弱み
	skills	技能
	difficulties	困難さ
	ideas / opinions	考え・意見
	solutions	解決策
	roles	役割

例

NPO specialists require many different skills. → 異なる技術について説明
Facilitating Fairtrade is important for many reasons. → 多くの理由について説明
Local farmers encounter several difficulties in getting decent wages.
→ いくつかの困難さについて説明

上記以外にも、説明する内容を示唆する語彙をリームに置くことで話題の展開を示唆できます。
Poverty can occur as a result of systemic discrimination.
→ 組織的な差別について説明

次のパラグラフ 1、2 の topic sentence としてもっとも適切なものを、それぞれ選択肢から選び
なさい。また、選んだ理由も説明しなさい。

1. _____ Farming in these areas has been sacrificed for the sake of
free trade and global industrialization. Firstly, the World Bank should cancel
Third World debt. Secondly, powerful countries need to cancel trade and farming
subsidies so that Third World countries can compete. Finally, NPOs can invest
in industries in Third World countries using local people and allowing them
ownership of businesses.

> **a.** A Japanese NPO visited Cambodia to explore an opportunity to improve
> current educational situations in the rural areas.
> **b.** In order to reduce the wealth gap between rich countries and poor countries,
> we need to introduce several approaches.
> **c.** The World Bank will have some significant roles in this century.

理由 : _____

2. _____ Farming in these areas has been sacrificed for the sake of free
trade and global industrialization. Big food companies are eager to seek profits and
are attempting to reduce the cost of production in the Third World. Some of them
ignore the working conditions in poor rural areas to win global competition.

> **a.** Agriculture business is important in throughout the world.
> **b.** Jason Fruits Company, based in the U.S., uses local labor paid the one-eighth
> of the wages of its home country.
> **c.** There are some reasons why we need to protect agriculture in developing
> countries.

理由 : _____

Task 4

次のパラグラフの topic sentence を、書き出しに続けて完成させなさい。

The mission of Fairtrade is _____

_____

The organization helps producers learn how to coordinate their production more effectively and deal with potential consumers. The group members educate customers to understand that they should provide a better deal for those that produce their food in undeveloped nations. They put the Fairtrade logo on recommended products indicating that the farmers have received a fair price

for their crop. The prices of Fairtrade goods tend to be relatively higher than those of international food firms. Yet, they appeal to consumers who are willing to take action to change the current unfair economic conditions. These people are happy to pay extra money in order to see a more sustainable society.

Task 5

次のパラグラフを完成させるために適切な topic sentence を書きなさい。

_____

_____

First, Fairtrade makes sure that farmers and workers receive a fair price plus a premium to improve their life in the community. Farmers get enough wages to support their families and pay for education for children. Additionally, the organization purchases products in a currency that is secure for the producer.

Therefore, locals do not have to take on the risk of currency fluctuation. Finally, Fairtrade attempts to establish long-term relationships with specific buyers. Producers can participate in the scheme to get a price that covers costs, no matter how low the market goes. Accordingly, Fairtrade can help producers plan for the future of sustainable production.

Task for Output 2

Writing about Sustainable Trade

In this chapter you have learned many things about why we can accept "fair prices" to enhance economic situations in developing countries. Write about your opinion regarding how to develop sustainable trade.

■ Outlining

以下のテンプレートを使って要点をまとめなさい。

Template 9 ■ Starting with Effective Introductory Statement	
Introductory sentence	
Topic sentence	

Subtopic 1
  Example
Subtopic 2
  Example	

Concluding sentence	

■ Write It Down: Write your opinion about sustainable trade.

ノートに英文で意見をまとめなさい。

■ Self-editing

1. 結束ができているか確認しなさい。
2. 適切にメタディスコースが使われているか確認しなさい。
3. 限定詞と主語と動詞の一致を確認しなさい。

■ Peer Review: Make some comments.

1. ペアの英文の Self-editing を確認しなさい。
2. ペアの英文を読んで、短いコメントを書きなさい。

_____

_____

_____

Focus on Accuracy : Modal Verbs

意味のよく似た助動詞

意味がよく似た助動詞であっても、使う際の意味が異なるものがあります。

■ will と be going to

	未来の予測	決断
will	漠然とした予測 Nobody knows how it **will** affect our community.	今決めた Nobody cooks? OK, then I **will** cook dinner.
be going to	何かの根拠のある予測 When we develop this medicine, people **are going to** live even longer.	以前から決まっていた I **am going to** a movie tonight. I got a ticket already.

■ must と have to
must　話し手の意志
　例　You **must** study hard in order to pass the examination.

have to　客観的にすべきことや、すでに決まりがある
　例　You **have to** follow the format when you submit assignments.

■ should と had better
should はあくまでもアドバイスで、それほど強制力はない
　例　Developing countries **should** follow the World Bank proposals.

had better は強制力があり must に近い表現になる
　例　The country **had better** follow the guidance of IMF.

■ would と used to
would は過去の行為で短期に行っていたこと
　例　We **would** go fishing every summer.

used to は過去の行為や習慣で長期的にあったこと
　例　We **used to** have a house in Oxford.

Topic: Traffic Congestion

11 SUSTAINABLE CITIES AND COMMUNITIES

Make cities and human settlements inclusive, safe, resilient and sustainable.

Chapter 8
Supporting Your Ideas

■ **Pre-Task :** Talk with your classmates about traffic jams.

✓ **Strategic Points** ··· Developing supporting sentences
　　　　　　　　　　　　Enhancing coherence by supporting the topic sentence

　You will learn how to write relevant supporting sentences to enhance topic sentences.

▶ この章で学ぶこと ▶ Topic sentence を効果的にサポートする方法
　　　　　　　　　 ▶ Supporting sentence の書き方

Strategic Focus 8: Developing Effective Supporting Sentences

パラグラフをより一貫性のあるものにするために、topic sentence に続く文を効果的に構築する必要があります。

━Task 1━

次の質問についてクラスメイトと話し合い、自分の回答も英語で書きなさい。

1. How long does it take to come to university in the morning?

_____

_____

2. How can we solve traffic congestion in big cities?

_____

_____

Writing Strategy 22 How to Write Supporting Sentences and Examples

Supporting sentence には３つのパターンがあります。

Pattern 1. Topic sentence の定義

means, is, be regarded as, refers to などの動詞句を使って定義する

Pattern 2. Topic sentence に関連する説明や理由、例示

・話題の展開に沿ってトピックを説明する

・理由を述べる This is because / ... because, / As

Pattern 3. Topic sentence の具体例

・For example, For instance などで始め、事例を示す

・証拠を示す

━Task 2━

1. 次のパラグラフの topic sentence に下線を引きなさい。

2. 続く supporting sentence が、上の３つのパターンのどれに該当するか答えなさい。

3. その根拠となる表現を抜き出して書きなさい。なお、一部の解答例が提示されています。

Automobile companies should follow a code of ethics for a sustainable society. It means that they should consider environmental issues when producing new cars. They need to reduce automobiles emitting poisonous exhaust in big cities. For example, they can develop innovative engines which can run on cleaner fuel or even natural gas.

	パターン	根拠となる表現
Supporting sentence 1	Pattern 1	
Supporting sentence 2		They need to reduce （＝ topic sentence に関連する説明）
Supporting sentence 3		For example

Task 3

次の topic sentence に続く supporting sentence を考え、3つずつ書きなさい。

1. There are several reasons I dislike commuting in the morning.

- _____
- _____
- _____

2. Public transportation has some advantages.

- _____
- _____
- _____

3. Public transportation has some disadvantages.

- _____
- _____
- _____

4. There are many benefits to having a small car.

- _____
- _____
- _____

Task 4

1. 次のパラグラフの各文がどのような Move に当てはまるか、解答欄にあわせて記入しなさい。
2. Supporting sentence が、Writing Strategy 22 で学んだ 3 つのパターンのどれに該当するか答えなさい。

⬇ DL 21   ◉ CD21

There are more than 10 million automobiles in several big cities in Asian countries. The problems facing road transport in these areas are numerous, and they have serious disadvantages for society. This means traffic congestion has a negative impact on our lives, such as increasing traffic accidents and pollution. First, the current road system cannot cope with the amount of traffic and increase in accidents. One major factor of the accidents is road stress which can again be due to traffic congestion. For example, dangerous driving on busy roads can raise the number of traffic accidents during rush hour. Second, using too many cars creates nitrogen oxides, other air pollutants and excessive noise. For instance, pollutants and noise levels are much higher than the world standards in big cities like Beijing and Delhi. To solve these problems, we have to reduce the number of cars or build new roads in cities.

Sentence 1: _____

Sentence 2: Topic sentence _____

Sentence 3: Supporting sentence, Pattern (1) _____

Sentence 4 & 5: (subtopic 1) Supporting sentences, Pattern ( ) ____

Sentence 6: (example) _____

Sentence 7: (subtopic 2) _____

Sentence 8: _____

Sentence 9: _____

Task for Output 1

Writing about Traffic Congestion

Task 4 のパラグラフを読んで、traffic congestion についての自分の意見をテンプレートを使って書きなさい。 ▶ **Template 7** [p. 43]

■ Self-editing

1. 結束ができているか確認しなさい。

2. 適切にメタディスコースが使われているか確認しなさい。

3. 限定詞と主語と動詞の一致を確認しなさい。

■ Peer Review: Make some comments.

1. ペアの英文の Self-editing を確認しなさい。

2. ペアの英文を読んで、短いコメントを書きなさい。

Writing Strategy 23 Coordinating Supporting Sentences

Topic sentence に続く supporting sentence と example の組み立て方には、主に以下の4つのパターンがあります。
1. 同じ観点から述べる　　**2.** 情報をつけ加える　　**3.** 対比する　　**4.** 反対の観点を述べる
Supporting sentence の前には、特徴的なメタディスコースをつけて組み立てを明示します。なお、必ずしも example の文を加える必要はありません。

1. 同じ観点から述べる

Firstly,	supporting sentence 1	example 1
Secondly,	supporting sentence 2	example 2
Finally,	supporting sentence 3	example 3

2. 情報をつけ加える

| supporting sentence 1 | | example 1 |

Besides, / In addition, / What is more, / Furthermore,

| supporting sentence 2 | | example 2 |

3. 対比する

Some | supporting sentence 1 | | example 1 |
Other(s) | supporting sentence 2 | | example 2 |

4. 反対の観点を述べる

| supporting sentence 1 | | example 1 |

In contrast, / On the other hand, / However,

| supporting sentence 2 | | example 2 |

Task for Output 2

Writing Opinion about the Congestion Charge

🎧 DL 22   💿 CD 22

London is like most big cities in the world. It's very congested and driving and travelling through the city can be very difficult. So, many people use the underground which is also known as the tube, or buses. Both are common ways of travelling. (1)However, the underground is expensive and not always very reliable. Sometimes the train stops and you don't know why, but Londoners get used to this.

To reduce traffic congestion by cars and improve public transportation, the government has introduced a new scheme. If you want to drive a car into the city of London, you have to pay 11.5 pounds in what is called the Congestion Charge. One effect of this is that lots of people are not using cars and they are using buses and the underground. (2)In addition, the benefit of this tax is that the government can spend more money on the underground and buses. The situation is getting better and the buses are now much better than before. The money is now being spent to improve the underground. Therefore, hopefully in the near future the underground will be a quick and reliable service.

■ Group Work:

このパラグラフの下線（1）、（2）はそれぞれ、Writing Strategy 23 の 4 つのパターンのどれが使われているか話し合いなさい。

Task for Output 3

🎧 DL 23　◎ CD23

Park and Ride

In many urban areas, traffic jams are becoming
larger and more frequent. On weekdays, city centers
are busy and always crowded with cars and buses.
It is very difficult for drivers to find a parking space
in the congested areas. To solve these problems,
Park & Ride schemes have been introduced in the

U.K. The purpose of this system is to reduce car usage and promote more sustainable
transport alternatives in the middle of towns. Local governments have developed big
car parking areas on the outskirts of city centers. Drivers visiting cities can park there
free of charge and get public buses toward city centers. The buses run frequently and
are comfortable for passengers. Although the bus fare itself is slightly expensive in
order to support this system, it is much cheaper than paying parking rates in the city
center. This system can reduce traffic congestion and the need for central parking
spaces. In addition, public transport has less of a negative impact on the environment
than taking a car.

■ *Group Work*

Park & Ride のシステムの利点について、クラスメイトと話し合いなさい。

■ *Write It Down*

以下の質問の回答を英語で書きなさい。

1. What do you think about the system?

_____

_____

_____

2. Is it possible to introduce the system in Japan? Why or why not?

_____

_____

_____

Task for Output 4

Problem-Solving for Traffic Problems

Template 10 は問題解決型のパラグラフの代表的なテンプレートです。これを活用して、この章で学んだ事例を使い、渋滞の問題とその解決策について書きなさい。

Template 10 ■ Problem-Solving Paragraph

Introductory sentence	
Topic sentence	
Problem 1 Solution 1	
Problem 2 Solution 2	
Concluding sentence	

Write It Down

ノートに英文で意見をまとめなさい。

Self-editing

1. 結束ができているか確認しなさい。

2. 適切にメタディスコースが使われているか確認しなさい。

3. 限定詞と主語と動詞の一致を確認しなさい。

Peer Review: Make some comments.

1. ペアの英文の Self-editing を確認しなさい。

2. ペアの英文を読んで、短いコメントを書きなさい。

_____

_____

Focus on Accuracy : Quantifiers

数量詞

■ エラーの多い数量詞表現

・可算名詞のみ使用

  few / a few, several, many, a (large / great) number of

・不可算名詞のみ使用

  little / a little, a bit of, much, a large amount of, a great deal of

・可算・不可算の両方が可能

  no, none, not any, some, any, most, a lot of, lots of, plenty of, all

■ 動詞が単数形になる数量詞

以下の数量詞が名詞句の主要部になると、動詞は単数になります。

例 **One** of my friends is a taxi driver.

      Each of his parents has a car.

      Either of them is able to help you.

      Much of his time is spent in the pub.

      Neither of the buses goes to the city center.

      Nothing has happened yet.

■ 動詞が複数形になる数量詞

例 **Many** of their drivers are fulltime workers.

      Several of our staff are bilingual speakers.

      Both candidates have great IT skills.

Quiz │ 次の英文における適切な動詞を選びなさい。

1. All of my money (is / are) missing.

2. Neither of them (is / are) ready for the interview.

3. Most of the work (is / are) easy.

4. Some jobs (is / are) difficult to get.

Topic: City and Environment

11 SUSTAINABLE CITIES AND COMMUNITIES

15 LIFE ON LAND

Make cities and human settlements inclusive, safe, resilient and sustainable.
Protect, restore and promote sustainable use of terrestrial ecosystems, sustainably manage forests, combat desertification, and halt and reverse land degradation and halt biodiversity loss.

Chapter 9
Concluding Paragraphs

■ **Pre-Task :** Talk with your classmates about restoring nature in the city.

☑ **Strategic Points** ⋯ Closing a paragraph
Enhancing reader's understanding

In this chapter, you will learn how to write an effective concluding sentence.

▶ この章で学ぶこと ▶ パラグラフの効果的な終わり方
▶ Concluding sentence の書き方

Strategic Focus 9: Concluding with an Effective Sentence

読者がパラグラフの理解を深め、内容を覚えられるような文を最後に書きます。

Task 1

次の質問についてクラスメイトと話し合い、自分の回答も英語で書きなさい。

1. Which do you like better, living in a big city or the countryside?

_____

_____

2. What are the disadvantages of living in a city?

_____

_____

Writing Strategy 24 Effective Concluding Sentence

・Concluding sentence でパラグラフの内容を再度アピール

復習のためパラグラフの構成を確認しましょう。図のように長めのパラグラフは、topic sentence の後に話題の展開の視点と関連する supporting sentence を書きます。内容が多くなる場合は読者に再度パラグラフの目的を明確に示すため、concluding sentence をまとめとして書くと効果的です。

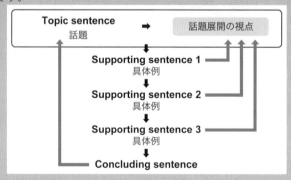

・Concluding sentence の3つのパターン

1. Topic sentence を別の表現で再度書く

代表的な書き出し　As I have argued ... / As discussed before ...

2. パラグラフの内容を要約する

代表的な書き出し　In summary / To summarize

3. 読者にパラグラフから示唆されることを伝える

代表的な書き出し　In conclusion / To conclude

⊨Task 2

次の各文は Writing Strategy 24 で示した concluding sentence の 3 つのパターンのうち、どれに当てはまるか答えなさい。また、選んだ理由も述べなさい。

a. In conclusion, I strongly suggest that we should plan for nature in the same way that we plan for building development. [　　]

理由：＿＿＿＿＿＿＿＿＿＿＿＿＿＿＿＿＿＿＿＿＿＿＿＿＿

b. In summary, educators and parents must facilitate awareness of environmental issues in the younger generations. [　　]

理由：＿＿＿＿＿＿＿＿＿＿＿＿＿＿＿＿＿＿＿＿＿＿＿＿＿

c. As I already mentioned, we are not alone on this planet. [　　]

理由：＿＿＿＿＿＿＿＿＿＿＿＿＿＿＿＿＿＿＿＿＿＿＿＿＿

⊨Task 3

次のパラグラフを読んで、パラグラフの concluding sentence として適切なものを選択肢から選びなさい。また、選んだ理由も述べなさい。

Input for Writing 1　

Tokyo Olympics

Nobody can deny that there are significant economic benefits to holding the world biggest sports events, such as the Olympics. However, developing many new buildings and sports facilities is not always good for the social environment. When Tokyo was chosen as the host city for the 2020 Olympics, many Japanese celebrated. Shortly after  that, a major British magazine *The Economist* ran a shocking article titled "Capital Crimes". The article was about the potential negative impact of the Tokyo Olympics on society. In particular, because space in a congested urban area is limited, there may be a need to destroy precious traditional architecture.

a. In summary, local people should share the benefits of the Olympic Games.

b. Therefore, holding the Olympic Games will significantly enhance the Japanese economy.

c. It can be said that we should avoid unnecessary development and preserve precious heritages.

理由：＿＿＿＿＿＿＿＿＿＿＿＿＿＿＿＿＿＿＿＿＿＿＿＿＿

Task for Output 1

Task 3 のパラグラフを読んで、自分の意見をテンプレートを使って書きなさい。

▶ **Template 7** [p. 43]

_____

_____

_____

_____

_____

_____

_____

■ *Self-editing*

1. 結束ができているか確認しなさい。

2. 適切にメタディスコースが使われているか確認しなさい。

3. 限定詞と主語と動詞の一致を確認しなさい。

■ *Peer Review:* Make some comments.

1. ペアの英文の Self-editing を確認しなさい。

2. ペアの英文を読んで、短いコメントを書きなさい。

_____

_____

Task 4

次のパラグラフに concluding sentence を書き加えなさい。

1. We need to cope with the problem of urbanization. It refers to a process whereby the population shifts from rural areas to urban areas. The increase in the population in cities causes rapid changes in the social infrastructure. The government needs to build more homes, business areas and transport links as more people begin living and working in central areas. Those movements are directed to continuous restructuring of architectures and destruction of nature.

_____

_____

2. It was necessary to set up some organization for environmental and heritage conservation in U.K. There are a great number of historic houses and ancient monuments in gardens and parks. They are valuable heritage sites to be protected for future generations. However, many are unable to pay for their own permanent preservation. They have to manage high maintenance costs and inheritance taxes. In some cases, the owners may give up owning the places and sell them to property developers. These companies tend to construct new hotels and residential areas to increase their profit.

_____

_____

_____

3. To protect historic places and nature, we need to introduce some schemes which are beneficial for every party. One example is the National Trust founded in 1895. It is an independent charity organization for environmental and heritage conservation in the U.K. Their activities have been authorized by the government since the National Trust Act 1907. When the owners of large private properties are no longer able to afford maintenance, they can donate the estate to the trust. The organization prevents land being sold off or mortgaged in order to preserve its original context. If people become members or donate money to the National Trust, they can expect tax reductions from the government. The trust members are entitled to free entry to more than 500 trust properties, including the childhood home of John Lennon. Members can participate in protecting many generous gifts of rural beauty and historic interest.

_____

_____

_____

Task for Output 2

1. 次のパラグラフに concluding sentence を書き加えなさい。　 DL 25　CD25

A Solution for Peter Rabbit?

Somebody should take actions to look after special places in nature forever, for everyone. In this case we may owe a lot to rabbits. Peter Rabbit, a beloved character, was created by Beatrix Potter. She lived in Hill Top Farm in the Lake District which had outstanding natural beauty. Beatrix was inspired by the unique beautiful surroundings and wrote wonderful stories for children. In them, Peter and Benjamin, named after Potter's pet rabbits, have great adventures around villages in Hill Top. Potter strongly hoped to maintain the local scenes which inspired the illustrations for her tales. She worried that the land would be irrecoverably ruined by development. After her great success, she worked closely with the National Trust and invested her fortune in land and the local community in the Lake District.

_____

_____

2. この章のすべてのパラグラフを読んで、都市開発と自然の保護に関する自分の意見の Outline を書きなさい。

Template 11 ■ Opinion Building	
Introductory sentence	
Topic sentence	In my opinion,
Problems	1. 2.
Solutions	1. 2.
Concluding sentence with opinion	

◼ *Write It Down*

自分の outline を活用して英文で意見をまとめなさい。

_____

_____

_____

_____

_____

_____

_____

_____

_____

_____

_____

◼ *Self-editing*

1. 結束ができているか確認しなさい。
2. 適切にメタディスコースが使われているか確認しなさい。
3　限定詞と主語と動詞の一致を確認しなさい。

◼ *Peer Review:* Make some comments.

1. ペアの英文の Self-editing を確認しなさい。
2. ペアの英文を読んで、短いコメントを書きなさい。

_____

_____

_____

Focus on Accuracy : Infinitives or Gerunds

不定詞と動名詞の選択

　特定の動詞によって、後に不定詞のみ、動名詞のみ、あるいは両方を目的語にとるものがあります。

■不定詞
次のような未来の事象を予測させる動詞は、一般に不定詞が目的語になります。
　hope, want, wish, expect（これから起こることへの期待や願望）
　promise（これからの行動の約束）
　plan（これからの行為を計画する）
　decide（これからの行為を決定する）
　agree（これからの行動に合意する）
　refuse（これからの行動を拒否する）

■動名詞
次の動詞が、動名詞のみが目的語になる代表的なものです。
　make, enjoy, quit, finish, escape, postpone, deny, avoid, miss

動詞の成句は、多くが動名詞のみが目的語となります。
　give up, put off, look forward to

■不定詞・動名詞の両方が目的語になるが意味が異なるもの

未来と過去の事象が目的語になるもの	
不定詞［未来の事象］	動名詞［過去の事象］
remember to（することを覚えている）	remember -ing（したことを覚えている）
forget to（することを忘れる）	forget -ing（したことを忘れる）
regret to（残念ながら～する）	regret -ing（したことを後悔する）

意味が特に異なるもの	
stop to（～するために立ち止まる）	stop -ing（～することを止める）
try to（～を努力する）	try -ing（試しにやってみる）

Topic:
Education for Future

4 QUALITY EDUCATION

Ensure inclusive and equitable quality education and promote lifelong learning opportunities for all.

Chapter 10
Comparison and Contrast Paragraphs

Pre-Task : Talk with your classmates about your university life.

Strategic Points ⋯ Three different types of comparison and contrast paragraphs

　This chapter explains how to organize different types of comparison and contrast paragraphs.

この章で学ぶこと ▶ 比較や対照を行う表現方法
　　　　　　　　 ▶ 3つのタイプの比較や対照パラグラフの構成

Strategic Focus 10: Comparison and Contrast Paragraphs

比較や対照を行うには、比べる内容を公平に並べます。

Task 1

次の質問についてクラスメイトと話し合い、自分の回答も英語で書きなさい。

1. How many books have you read since you entered university?

_____

_____

2. How many hours do you spend for studying before and after lectures at university?

_____

_____

Writing Strategy 25 3 Types of Compare and Contrast Paragraphs

comparison は類似点を述べることで、contrast は相違点を述べることです。例えば A と B の異なる事象を比較する際には、以下の３つの方法があります。
※それぞれの構成によって比較対照の焦点が変わります。

Format 1: A の全体の観点から述べる ➡ B の全体の観点から述べる

Format 2: A と B の共通の観点を述べる ➡ A と B の相違の観点を述べる

共通点　　 | A　　　　B |
↓
相違点　　 | A　　　　B |

Format 3: 項目ごとの観点から比較する（例えば３つの項目で比較する場合）

　　　　・１つ目の類似や相違　　・２つ目の類似や相違　　・３つ目の類似や相違

項目１　 | A　　　　B |
↓
項目２　 | A　　　　B |
↓
項目３　 | A　　　　B |

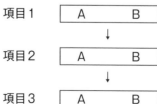

Task 2

次のそれぞれの比較方法はどのような観点に焦点を当てているでしょうか。空所に適切な語句を書き入れなさい。

1. 英国の教育について述べる ➡ 日本の教育について述べる

   （　　　　　　）の観点を重視

2. 英国と日本の共通点を述べる ➡ 英国と日本の相違点を述べる

   （　　　　　　）の観点を重視

3. 英国と日本の学生生活ごとに比較する

   ・勉強時間の類似や相違　・アルバイトの類似や相違　・就職活動の類似や相違

   （　　　　　　）の観点を重視

Task 3

Brainstorming

次の表は米国と日本の大学生の生活を比較したものです。左の米国を参照して右の日本の欄を記入しましょう。

American University Life Memo

- A lot of assignments
  Writing 2-3 essays a week
- Reading many books
  Reading 2-3 books a week
- Heavy use of library
  Libraries open 24 hours
- Strict Attendance
  If you miss two lectures, you may have to drop out.
- Serious lecturers
  They prepare a lot for lessons
  Giving precise feedback on student assignments
- Very difficult to graduate
- High cost
  Average total cost of a private school is $46,950 per year
  Top university tuition: $50,000 per year
- Doing part-time jobs
  Working at cafés and restaurants
- Accommodations
  Majority of students live on campus
- Enjoying social activities
  Joining a club

Japanese University Life Memo

─Task 4─

Task 3 の米国と日本で対応する項目から、自分が重要だと思う観点を 3 つほど選び、Writing Strategy 25 で示した Format 2 と 3 に該当するそれぞれのリストを完成させなさい。

Format 2: A と B の共通点を述べる ➡ A と B の相違点を述べる

・1 つの共通点と 2 つの相違点を選ぶ

共通点：(　　　　　　　　　　　　　　　　　　　　　)

例 _____

相違点 1：(　　　　　　　　　　　　　　　　　　　　)

例 _____

相違点 2：(　　　　　　　　　　　　　　　　　　　　)

例 _____

Format 3: 項目ごとに比較する

・1 つ目の類似や相違　・2 つ目の類似や相違　・3 つ目の類似や相違

項目 1：(　　　　　　　　　　　　　　　　　　　　　)

例 _____

_____

項目 2：(　　　　　　　　　　　　　　　　　　　　　)

例 _____

_____

項目 3：(　　　　　　　　　　　　　　　　　　　　　)

例 _____

_____

Writing Strategy **26** Expressions for Comparison and Contrast

比較・対照をする際に以下のような表現がよく使われます。
・ 節を結ぶ contrast 表現
・ 文やパラグラフをつなぐ表現
・ パラグラフの構成に役立つメタディスコース

・節を結ぶ contrast 表現
　　等位接続詞：[A] but [B] / [A] yet [B]
　　従属接続詞：Although [A], [B] 「A にも関わらず、B である」
　　　　　　　　While [A], [B] 「A である一方、B である」
　　　　　　　　Whereas [A], [B] 「A である一方、B である」

・文やパラグラフをつなぐ表現
　　■ Comparison: Like / Likewise / Similarly / In the same ... 「同様に」
　　■ Contrast: However 「しかしながら」
　　　　　　　　In contrast / On the other hand 「反対に」

・パラグラフの構成に役立つメタディスコース
　　■ Comparison
　　　　Topic sentence: There are ... similarities / One similarity is / Another similarity is
　　■ Contrast
　　　　Topic sentence: There are ... differences / One difference is / Another difference is

─Task 5

次の英文中にある比較の表現と、比較の内容を確認しなさい。

Surprising Fact

About 60 percent of U.S. university students study more than 11 hours a week. On the other hand, only about 15 percent of students study more than 11 hours a week in Japan.

■ *Group Work:* Let's discuss.

Why do you think American students seem to be more serious about their studies than Japanese students?

Task for Output 1

Writing Strategy 25 で示した Format 2 を使い、米国と日本の大学生活を比較する英文を次の書き出しに続けて書きなさい。

    There are both similarities and differences in college life in the U.S. and Japan. Students in both countries are similar in terms of _____

_____

_____

    There are also differences. At American universities, _____

_____

_____

_____ , in Japan _____

_____

_____

Task for Output 2

 DL 26　 CD 26

Education in Developing Countries

    When France colonized Laos, it introduced the French educational system, which only focused on members of the upper class. As it was operated in the French language and not provided for ordinary Lao people, Laotians had only a few opportunities to get an education. Since 1975, the Lao government has gradually improved the education system. However, they can spend very little on education because of financial problems. Laos is one of the poorest countries in Asia. The government cannot provide teaching materials or adequate textbooks to all pupils. The conditions in rural areas are worse than in cities. Some children still do not attend school or drop out at a very young age. In such places, schools are often far away and most children are always expected to work on their families' farms. Large families cannot afford to support every child and have to choose which children go to school. Most schools are poorly constructed of bamboo and thatch with no walls or roof. As opportunities for teacher training are limited and conditions are poor, including low wages, there are not enough qualified teachers.

◼ *Write It Down*

前のページの英文を読んで、日本の教育環境と比較する英文をノートに書きなさい。

◼ *Self-editing*

1. 結束ができているか確認しなさい。

2. 適切にメタディスコースが使われているか確認しなさい。

3. 主語と動詞の一致を確認しなさい。

◼ *Peer Review:* Make some comments.

1. ペアの英文の Self-editing を確認しなさい。

2. ペアの英文を読んで、短いコメントを書きなさい。

Your essay is _____

_____

Because _____

_____

_____

Focus on Accuracy : Noun Usage

間違いやすい名詞

　ライティングでは名詞の使い方のエラーも多くみられます。特に多いのが、可算名詞（countable noun）と不可算名詞（uncountable noun）の違いです。可算名詞は一般的に複数を表す時に語尾を変化させます。一方不可算名詞は、語尾の変化はありません。ここではエッセイコーパスで使用頻度が高く、学習者にエラーの多い名詞に注目します。

■ 不規則に変化する可算名詞

種類	単数（左）－ 複数（右）
単数・複数が同形	fish － fish, sheep － sheep, deer － deer, series － series, species － species
語尾が o で es を付加	potato － potatoes, tomato － tomatoes
語尾の f/fe を ves に変形	half － halves, knife － knives, life － lives, loaf － loaves, wife － wives
語尾の is を es に変形	analysis － analyses, crisis － crises, diagnosis － diagnoses, oasis － oases, thesis － theses
oo を ee に変形	foot － feet, goose － geese, tooth － teeth
その他	child － children, man － men, woman － women, mouse － mice, person － people, criterion － criteria, phenomenon － phenomena, datum － data

■ 不可算名詞の物質名詞を入れ物（container）などに入れて数える

不可算名詞	単数（左）－ 複数（右）
water, beer	a glass of － two glasses of a bottle of － two bottles of
sugar, salt	a spoon of － three spoons of
spaghetti	a packet of － four packets of
soup	a can of － two cans of
soap	a bar of － two bars of
cake	a piece of － two pieces of
paper	a sheet of － two sheets of

■ 目に見えない概念の抽象名詞を、特定の活動や、その結果として数える

名詞	不可算名詞	可算名詞
analysis	分析という概念	特定の分析
business	商業全般	特定の商業活動
change	変化	変化した事象
experience	一般的な経験	特定の経験
industry	産業全般	特定の産業
influence	一般的な影響	具体的な影響
opinion	意見全般	特定の意見
performance	行動全般	具体的な活動

■ 可算と不可算で意味が変わるもの

名詞	不可算名詞	可算名詞
interest	興味・関心	利益・利害

Part 3

Strategies for Essays and Academic Papers

Part 3 ではエッセイの書き方や、
論文執筆に向けた基礎を学びます。

Topic:
Decent Job

8 DECENT WORK AND ECONOMIC GROWTH

Promote sustained, inclusive and sustainable economic growth, full and productive employment and decent work for all.

Chapter 11
Essay Structure

Pre-Task : Talk with your classmates about your future career.

Strategic Points ⋯ Introduction, Body, Conclusion
Thesis statement

This chapter deals with how to develop a persuasive essay.

この章で学ぶこと ▶ 読みやすいエッセイの構成
▶ Thesis statement の書き方

Strategic Focus 11: Developing an Effective Essay

英文エッセイでは、読者が内容を理解しやすいように Introduction, Body,
Conclusion の3つの Move を構築します。

─Task 1─

職業について話し合い、自分の将来について書きなさい。

■ *Group Work:* Ask your classmates the following questions.

1. What kind of job would you like to have in the future?
2. What is important to you in deciding on a career?

■ *Write It Down*

自分の興味ある仕事について短いパラグラフを書きなさい。

In the future, I would like to _____

_____

_____

Writing Strategy **27** Essay Format 1: Introduction

英文エッセイは Introduction, Body, Conclusion の3つのパートで構成します。ここでは1
つ目のパート、Introduction の Move を構築するストラテジーを確認します。

・Introduction（序論）：以下の3つの Move で構成します。
Move 1：読者の興味の喚起　　Move 2：読む目的の明示と内容の示唆　　Move 3：論文構成の提示

Move 1：読者の興味の喚起

　Chapter 7 の Writing Strategy 20（p. 55）で示したように、以下の5つのストラテジーから選
択します。

1. 一般的な事象の把握から始める
2. 多くの権威者や研究者が重要な話題と認識していることを示す
3. 興味深い逸話から始める
4. 歴史的な背景を述べる
5. 統計などの数字を使い、議論する課題の重要性や普遍性を訴える

Move 2：読む目的の明示と内容の示唆

　エッセイ全体の topic sentence となります。課題の重要さを述べ、それに対してどのような観
点から議論をしていくのかを示し、読むための目的を明確にします。

Move 3 : 論文構成の提示

　論文の主題（thesis statement）を書き、長めのエッセイの場合には構成を明示します。課題を、いかなる観点から議論をするのか示します。どのような構成で読んでいくのか、事前に読者に内容を予想させ、読みやすくします。基本的には、この場所に、次のストラテジーで示すボディの各パラグラフにおけるtopic sentenceそれぞれの話題をまとめ、要約しておくと分かりやすい構成となります。

■　資格試験や大学の授業の課題には主に３つのタイプのエッセイがあり、それぞれの論文構成の提示に特徴があります。

Type 1: 意見を述べる　➡　まず課題に対する自分の立場を明確にし、その理由を議論していく

Type 2: 比較対照を行う　➡　２つの見解を比べ、それぞれの特徴を述べ、長所や短所を議論する

Type 3: 問題解決をする　➡　どのような観点から問題を解決していくのか述べる

─Task 2 ─

次の英文は Writing Strategy 27 で示した Introduction の３つの Move のうち、どれに該当するか答えなさい。また、その理由も述べなさい。

1. In this essay I will discuss in detail about why we need teachers in terms of enhancing social skills of learners.
   Move [　] 理由 : ＿＿＿＿＿＿＿＿＿＿＿＿＿＿＿＿＿＿＿

2. The Ministry of Education recently reports that computers could replace teachers, some of whom might be made redundant.
   Move [　] 理由 : ＿＿＿＿＿＿＿＿＿＿＿＿＿＿＿＿＿＿＿

3. There is little doubt that AI will be more prevalent in our classrooms. However, I believe such technology cannot take over the teacher's role as facilitator in the learning context.
   Move [　] 理由 : ＿＿＿＿＿＿＿＿＿＿＿＿＿＿＿＿＿＿＿

─Task 3 ─

次の英文は Writing Strategy 27 で示した Introduction の３つのタイプのエッセイのうちどれに該当するか、対応する論文構成の提示を確認して答えなさい。また、その理由も述べなさい。

1. In this essay I will discuss some of the positive and negative aspects of animal testing.
   Type [　] 理由 : ＿＿＿＿＿＿＿＿＿＿＿＿＿＿＿＿＿＿＿

2. I agree with this point of view for the following three reasons.
   Type [　] 理由 : ＿＿＿＿＿＿＿＿＿＿＿＿＿＿＿＿＿＿＿

3. We have good solutions to encourage the use of public transport in urban cities and decrease dependence on cars.
   Type [　] 理由 : ＿＿＿＿＿＿＿＿＿＿＿＿＿＿＿＿＿＿＿

Writing Strategy **28** Essay Format 2: Body and Conclusion

・Body（本論）

Introduction で示した thesis statement の内容を、次の手順で３つ位のパラグラフに分けて詳細に説明します。

・ ３つ位の観点でエッセイの主題をサポートする

・ それぞれの観点ごとにパラグラフをまとめる

・ 必要に応じて各 supporting sentence や example で説明する

・Conclusion（結論）

エッセイの結論は次のように構成します。

1. Paragraph 1-3 をまとめる

2. 結語を述べ、普遍的な議論や提案をする

以下はエッセイの構成をまとめた図です。

Move 1 Introduction
・読者の興味の喚起：論文の価値を訴える
・読む目的の明示：話題を明確に定義する
・論文構成の提示：論文の主題を示す

Move 2 Body

Paragraph 1
Topic sentence　話題→話題展開の視点

Supporting sentence 1　Example
Supporting sentence 2　Example
Supporting sentence 3　Example

Concluding sentence

（Supporting sentence の数や Example の記述は書き手が選択する）

Paragraph 2
Paragraph 3

Move 3 Conclusion
・Paragraph 1-3 をまとめる
・結語を述べ、普遍的な議論や提案をする

次の英文は Conclusion のパラグラフです。最も適切な順番になるよう、並べ替えなさい。ただしすべてを大文字で始めています。

1. In conclusion, → [　　] → [　　] → [　　]

    a. We can replace many of them by using an alternative such as computer-based simulations.

    b. Some scientists still use animals to test the safety of newly developed drugs.

    c. However, we should reduce such experiments as soon as possible.

2. To conclude, → [　　] → [　　] → [　　]

    a. By increasing the use of such public transport, we can reduce congestion on city streets.

    b. We immediately need to take such actions to reduce air pollution and make urban living more comfortable.

    c. We should make trains and buses more convenient in order to attract more commuters.

Task for Output 1

次のページのエッセイの Body をよく読み、以下の Surprising Facts を参考にして Introduction と Conclusion をノートに書きなさい。なお、各 Body の topic sentence には下線を引いてあります。

Surprising Facts about Japan

· Japan's relative poverty rate was fourth highest among the 30 OECD countries in the mid-2000s.

· The average full-time workers' salary is ¥4,870,000 and that of non-full timers is ¥1,720,000.

· The percentage of temporary workers increased from 30% in 2001 to 37.8% in 2017.

Title: Mind the Widening Income Gap

Introduction（＝ノートにまとめてください）

Body

1.  DL 27 CD27

One of the problems is due to misinterpretation of the government about enhancing the flexible labor market in Japan. The International Labor Organization (ILO) suggested providing more jobs by making use of temporary staffing industries and dispatching workers. The main purpose was to improve the unemployment rate in European countries where job flexibility and mobility had already been established. By following the ILO suggestion, in 1999 the Japanese government eased the Worker Dispatch Law set in 1985 which regulated the extra-legal system of subcontractor personnel dispatching that had once caused problems in manufacturing industries. Traditionally the Japanese government supports development of major private industries and expects them to look after employees until retirement, giving them a decent pension and other benefits. In order to protect such company-centered social welfare systems, the government regulated laying off and discouraged temporary employment. However, because of the long-term recession, the traditional whole-life employment system did not work well. To solve the economic stagnation, politicians thought they should remake the system to create a more dynamic labor market. In this system, not all jobs are held for life and people can enjoy the benefit of job

mobility. Unfortunately, the government plan did not work at all. This is because they could not find an appropriate way to develop the new system. It was also difficult to break the long tradition of seeking stability within the same workplace. As a result, it only increased the number of temporary workers who are used in conditions inferior to those of full-time staff.

2.  DL 28 CD28

The second turning point was the easing of the labor law in 2004 under the administration introducing American-style deregulation. Through this change, temporary workers can work on factory lines and in other jobs once largely restricted to full-time workers. In particular, automobile and electronics industries can use temporary employees with low wages and enjoy the benefits of the reform. These industries have been driving forces for Japanese economic development through exporting reliable goods with reasonable prices. However, because of global competition, other countries such as South Korea and China have dramatically expanded the global supply of high-quality and low-cost products. Japanese companies gradually lost in competition against newcomers. The industry leaders of big business claimed that Japan's high labor cost is the problem and it should be reduced. The economic advisor of the administration was in favor of the deregulation of the American way. He persuaded the prime minister to support the business lobbyists. Finally, the ban on worker dispatching for manufacturing jobs was lifted. Thanks to this deregulation in 2004, Japanese companies' total ordinary profit almost doubled from 2001 to 2006. In 2007, manufacturing industries became able to extend the period of employing dispatch workers to three years. It could be said that private firms could enjoy the benefit of easing the laws. On the other hand, the number of non-fulltime workers increased by about 4.5 million. In sum, the deregulation supported major industries but not the ordinary people in terms of working conditions.

3.   🎧 DL 29   💿 CD29

The final stroke was caused by the financial crisis of 2008. It has revealed the negative impact of deregulation on the labor market. A series of financial problems starting with the bankruptcy of Lehman Brothers in the U.S.A. caused damage all over the world. In particular, as many Japanese manufacturing industries heavily depend on the American market, they suffered from the serious recession. Thanks to the government reform of the Labor Law, these companies held many dispatch workers. They could start terminating contracts with workers in fragile situations. According to the Labor Ministry, 131,000 people were laid off between October 2008 and March 2009. The majority of them were temporary workers who were sent by staffing agencies or hired on short-term contracts. Big companies gradually recovered from the difficult conditions. The total ordinary profit almost doubled from 2009 to 2016 and their financial situations have become very stable. However, the companies decreased the number of full-time staff and increased that of temporary workers. Many companies save their profits in-house or spend them for overseas M & A. They seem to have become reluctant to invest money in human resources, which was once regarded as the most important asset of a company.

Conclusion (＝ノートにまとめてください)

■ *Self-editing*

1. 結束ができているか確認しなさい。
2. 適切にメタディスコースが使われているか確認しなさい。
3. 主語と動詞の一致を確認しなさい。

■ *Peer Review:* Make some comments.

1. ペアの英文の Self-editing を確認しなさい。
2. ペアの英文を読んで、短いコメントを書きなさい。

_____

_____

_____

Task for Output 2

日本の格差社会に関する自分の意見をノートに英文で書きなさい。Introduction, Body, Conclusion
を書き、エッセイとして完成させなさい。

Focus on Accuracy : Use of Adjectives and Adverbs

形容詞と副詞の用法

■ 使役動詞・知覚動詞は形容詞を補語とする

誤 He makes me <u>happily</u>.　　正 He makes me **happy**.

誤 My mother let me be <u>freely</u>.　　正 My mother let me be **free**.

誤 Jane looks <u>cheerfully</u>.　　正 Jane looks **cheerful**.

誤 It sounds <u>strangely</u>.　　正 It sounds **strange**.

■ 間違いやすい副詞

・hard は形容詞と副詞が同じ形です。hardly は、「ほとんどない」という副詞です。

誤 In order to pass the examination, he studies very <u>hardly</u>.

正 In order to pass the examination, he studies very **hard**.

・fast は形容詞と副詞が同じ形です。fastly は、「しっかりと」という副詞です。

誤 To win the race, Lucy ran very <u>fastly</u>.

正 To win the race, Lucy ran very **fast**.

・late は「遅く」という意味の形容詞で、lately は、「最近」という意味の副詞になります。

誤 Have you seen Jane <u>late</u>?

正 Have you seen Jane **lately**?

■ Almost と Most

・Almost は副詞で、Most は形容詞なので間違いやすい語彙です。

誤 <u>Almost</u> children love Disneyland.

正 **Most** children love Disneyland.

Most of the children love Disneyland.

Almost all children love Disneyland.

Topic:
Eco-friendly

12 RESPONSIBLE CONSUMPTION AND PRODUCTION

Ensure sustainable consumption and production patterns.

Chapter 12
Problem-Solving Essay

■ **Pre-Task :** Talk with your classmates about eco-friendly activities you do.

☑ **Strategic Points** ⋯ Providing solutions and relating benefits

This chapter deals with how to develop a persuasive essay.

▶ この章で学ぶこと ▶ 問題解決のエッセイの書き方

Strategic Focus 12: Providing Solutions

課題を明確にし、解決方法をわかりやすく伝えます。また、その解決方法のメリットを読者に説明します。

Task 1

1と2の質問についてクラスメイトと話し合いなさい。その後、自分の回答を英語で書きなさい。

1. Do you know any examples of pollution problems in Japan? For example?
2. Which problems caused by industrial waste disposal do you think are most serious in Japan?
3. 2の質問に対する回答について少し詳しい説明を書きなさい。

_____

_____

_____

Writing Strategy 29 Providing Solutions

問題を解決するエッセイは以下の5つの Move が重要になります。

Move 1: 問題を正確に簡潔に述べる

Move 2: 問題の定義を行う

    ・なぜそれが問題なのか詳しく述べる

    ・他の問題とどのように違うのか

Move 3: 問題の理由や原因を明確にする

Move 4: 問題の解決方法を示す

Move 5: 解決方法の利点を明確にする。または解決方法の実行を訴える

　問題の解決にはそれを理解する知識や、案をまとめる調査が必要となります。そのためにはまず、問題を正確に把握し、その原因や起こった影響を調べます。次に、その解決策を見つけます。インターネットなどで検索することもできますが、それは既に誰かが提案したもので独自性はあまりありません。読者をより強く説得するには、オリジナルの価値のある解決策を示すことが重要になります。このためには、新聞や書籍などで公刊資料を調べ、問題の根源を深く理解する必要があります。

Task 2

次の各文は問題解決の英文を並べ替えたものです。Writing Strategy 29 を参考にして適切な Move 順に並べ替えなさい。また、各文が5つの Move のうち、どれに該当するか答えなさい。さらに、その根拠となる箇所に下線を引きなさい。

・適切な順番：**a** → ___ → ___ → ___ → ___

a. As Japan achieved economic growth in the mid-1960s, the country faced serious air pollution. In particular, people living in big cities like Tokyo suffered from smog.   [Move 1]

b. The engineers of Honda Motor Company thought it was their mission to reduce smog in cities and bring back blue skies. Although the new technology for reduction of toxic emission gas was very challenging, they spent all of their energy developing a new engine to reduce harmful emissions. Finally, in 1972 they developed the CVCC engine which could drastically reduce toxic emissions.   [Move   ]

c. Japan entered the age of motorization, and the number of cars in large cities increased dramatically. At its worst, Tokyo was covered in smog around 300 days a year. Emissions from automobiles and other vehicles were major sources of smog. Therefore, it was essential to reduce the toxic emission gasses from automobiles. Not only Japan but also the American government decided to strictly regulate vehicle exhaust emissions such as CO and NOx. However, it was very difficult and expensive to develop low emission engine technology.   [Move   ]

d. The smog is especially harmful to children and senior citizens. It causes shortness of breath and pain. It also causes asthma. The main cause of pollution is toxic emissions from vehicles.   [Move   ]

e. Honda vehicles became the first to meet Japanese and United States emission standards. As the new technology reduced pollutants in exhaust and used less fuel, Honda championed it for the world. Other major car companies, such as Toyota, Ford, and Chrysler introduced Honda's system. Accordingly, the number of days with smog has gradually decreased in Japan and the U.S.   [Move   ]

Task for Output 1

Task 2の英文を読んで、企業が社会に果たす役割について自分の意見をノートに英文で書きなさい。

Self-editing

読みやすい英文か確認しなさい。

Peer Review: Make some comments.

ペアの英文を読んでコメントを書きなさい。

_____

_____

_____

Writing Strategy 30 Kinds of Solutions

５種類の解決方法

問題や課題の解決には、以下のような様々な手法があります。読者にどの解決策の手法を最終的に訴えたいのか選んでから書き始めましょう。

1. 問題の原因を取りのぞく
2. 問題を改善するものや手段を加える
3. 問題を解決する新たなシステムや枠組みを提案する
4. 政府や行政に改善を訴える
5. 問題を気づかせ誘導する

☐ 問題を見つける

1. まずは身近な例で自分が不便に思うことや、困っていること、関心のあることをリストアップします。エッセイの内容を深めるためには、社会的な問題と関連のあるテーマを選ぶと、読者によりアピールしやすくなります。このため SDGs を参照してテーマを絞るとよいでしょう。
2. Brainstorming により、それらの原因や問題点、関連する人や場所を自由に書きだします。
3. Cluster map を作成します。

☐ 問題解決エッセイの注意点

・読者にとっても重要な課題である点を訴えます。
・解決策は、以下の点を考慮に入れて読者を説得します。
  1. 容易に導入できる
  2. 問題の解決に最も適している
  3. 効率よく解決できる

─Task 3─

次の各文は Writing Strategy 30 で示した５種類の解決方法のうち、どれに該当するか、その理由も述べ答えなさい。

a. It is important to educate tourists by enhancing participation in eco-tourism.
[   ] 理由：＿＿＿＿＿＿＿＿＿＿＿＿＿＿＿＿＿＿＿＿＿＿＿＿＿

b. We should suggest making a law to protect major sources of drinking water.
[   ] 理由：＿＿＿＿＿＿＿＿＿＿＿＿＿＿＿＿＿＿＿＿＿＿＿＿＿

c. We must introduce heavier penalties for illegal dumping of industrial waste.
[   ] 理由：＿＿＿＿＿＿＿＿＿＿＿＿＿＿＿＿＿＿＿＿＿＿＿＿＿

d. Instead of nuclear power generation, more cost-effective and safe renewable energy should be developed.
[   ] 理由：＿＿＿＿＿＿＿＿＿＿＿＿＿＿＿＿＿＿＿＿＿＿＿＿＿

e. We had better stop unnecessary animal testing for developing cosmetic products.
[   ] 理由：＿＿＿＿＿＿＿＿＿＿＿＿＿＿＿＿＿＿＿＿＿＿＿＿＿

Writing Strategy *31* Two Formats for Problem-Solving Essay

問題解決型のエッセイには以下の２つのフォーマットがあります。
1. 問題と解決をまとめて記述
2. 各問題と解決をそれぞれ記述

1. 問題と解決をまとめて記述

Introduction
Body 1: ３つ位の問題を順に記述
Body 2: ３つ位の解決策を順に記述
Conclusion

2. 各問題と解決をそれぞれ記述

Introduction
Body 1: 問題１と解決方法１
Body 2: 問題２と解決方法２
Body 3: 問題３と解決方法３
Conclusion

次の Reference を参考に Introduction に続けて Body と Conclusion を書き、問題解決のエッセイを完成させなさい。この際、Writing Strategy 31 のどちらかのフォーマットを使いなさい。

Reference

DL 30　　CD30

　　The problem with plastic pollutants is that currently only 9% is being recycled. Much plastic is being left to leak into rivers and oceans. As plastic takes about 400 years to decompose, most of it ends up polluting the oceans. However, according to a survey, while many Japanese understand the importance of being eco-friendly, they do not have any clear ideas on what to do. Accordingly, it is not easy to educate consumers about what they should do to protect the environment and why it matters. One example of effective consumer communication regarding the natural environment is Coca-Cola Japan's cutting-edge marketing success with I LOHAS. Until recently, mainly imported mineral water products were sold in Japan. Most of the imported products utilized blue bottles and labels to symbolize fresh water, while advertising focused on connecting the products to beautiful scenes of nature. I LOHAS on the other hand took a very different approach. This brand focused on the eco-friendliness of the product by suggesting customers the way to join activities for enhancing the environment. Company engineers invented a thin plastic material that was 40 percent lighter than conventional PET bottles. Empty I LOHAS bottles can be easily twisted and crushed to a smaller size. This means that every time someone buys I LOHAS water rather than a competing product, they are aiding the environment because the empty bottle reduces the amount of space and cost needed for recycling. In line with the eco-friendly nature of this product, green is used for the cap and label. TV commercials have a famous actor demonstrate the ease with which the bottles are crushed and encourages consumers to buy I LOHAS and care about eco-friendliness. This eco-friendly campaign has brought great success to I LOHAS. Over 2 billion bottles were shipped during the first 3.5 years of sales, and growth expanded abroad to new markets such as South Korea, Thailand and Singapore.

Introduction

 DL31 CD31

    There has been a rapid and extreme increase in production of plastic products such as PET bottles. Researchers predict that the amount of plastic produced in 2019 will double by 2030. It will mean more trash and increase the amount of plastics in oceans. The solution for beverage companies is to encourage customers to recycle PET bottles more actively and improve the recycling system. This essay reports how Coca-Cola Japan successfully decreased production of plastic pollutants by focusing on innovation and marketing efforts.

Body

_____

_____

_____

_____

_____

_____

_____

_____

_____

_____

_____

_____

Conclusion

_____

_____

_____

_____

_____

_____

_____

◼ *Self-editing*

読みやすい英文か確認しなさい。

◼ *Peer Review:* Make some comments.

ペアの英文を読んでコメントを書きなさい。

_____

_____

_____

Task for Output 3

今度は、Writing Strategy 31（p. 103）のもう一つのフォーマットで Body を完成させなさい。

_____

_____

_____

_____

_____

_____

_____

_____

_____

_____

Focus on Accuracy : Conditionals

仮定法

■ 仮定法には主に5つのパターンがあります。

仮定法の種類	If 節の動詞	主節の動詞
未来の仮定	If ＋ 現在形 If it rains tomorrow,	未来形 we will not play tennis.
現在の仮定	If ＋ 現在形 If you have the membership,	現在形 all facilities here are available to you.
現在の事実に反する仮定	If ＋ 過去 If I were you,	would 原形 I would not behave like that.
過去の事実に反する仮定	If ＋ had 過去分詞 If I had studied hard,	would have 過去分詞 I would have passed the exam.
過去の事実に反する仮定が現在の状況に影響を与えている	If ＋ had 過去分詞 If I had passed the exam,	would 原形 I would be an accountant now.

■ 仮定法でよく使われる表現

・If it were not for… (もし～がないと) ／ If it had not been for… (もし～がなかったら)

例 **If it had not been for** the support from council officers, we would not have managed this problem.

この構文の If 節は But for や Without で書き換えができます。

例 **But for / Without** the support from council officers, we would not have managed this problem.

・I wish 過去形 / could 原形 ➡ この構文は叶わない願望を表現します。

例 **I wish** I **were** you.
I wish I **could play** tennis like him.

Topic: Reducing Inequality

5 GENDER EQUALITY

10 REDUCED INEQUALITIES

Achieve gender equality and empower all women and girls.
Reduce inequality within and among countries.

Chapter 13
The First Step for Academic Papers

- **Pre-Task :** Talk with your classmates about equality irrespective of disability or gender.

- **Strategic Points** ··· Introduction Move 1: Defining your research territory

  This chapter deals with how to define your research territory.

- この章で学ぶこと ▶研究論文の書き方の基礎と研究テーマの重要性の伝え方

Strategic Focus 13: Validating the Value of Your Research

最初に研究論文の構成を学びます。続いて論文の Introduction の章における研究価値の訴求方法を学びます。

Task 1

次の英文の質問についてクラスメイトと話し合い、自分の回答も書きなさい。

1. What is your main theme about your field of study?
2. Why do you think your topic is important?

3. 上の質問に関する回答を書きなさい。

Writing Strategy 32　Structure of Academic Paper

研究論文には決まったフォーマットがあり、タイムマルドラ（TAIMRDRA）という以下の
Move で構成します。

- **T**itle　論文のタイトル
- **A**bstract　論文要旨
- **I**ntroduction　序論
- **M**ethod　研究の実施方法
- **R**esult　研究結果の報告
- **D**iscussion　考察
- **R**eferences　参考文献
- **A**ppendix / Appendices　付表

・Title　論文のタイトル

　短く的確に研究内容を反映し、できるだけ読者の注意を引くタイトルをつけます。

・Abstract　論文要旨

　以下に示すIntroduction, Method, Result, Discussionをそれぞれ1文程度にまとめた構成にします。読む価値が特にあることを訴えます。Abstractの後に論文を反映するキーワード(keyword)を3〜5つ記載するとわかりやすくなります。

・Introduction　序論

　とても重要な章で、研究の設計図を示します。まず先行研究を活用して課題の重要性を述べます。さらに既存の論文の批評をし、研究テーマの新規性を訴えます。最後にそのテーマの課題をいかに克服したのか記載します。

・Method　研究の実施方法

　研究方法が妥当で信頼性があることを読者に伝えます。先行研究の代表的な手法を参考にして、データの収集の対象や、時期、方法などを詳細に書きます。他の研究者が同じ条件で、同じ実験などをできるように研究の再現性を明確にします。

・Result　研究結果の報告

　研究の結果を正確に伝えます。研究領域の先行研究を参考に、図や表を入れると分かりやすく、読み手にインパクトを与えます。

・Discussion　考察

　得られた結果の解釈を行います。該当する研究領域にどのような貢献をしたのか、具体的に述べます。イントロダクションで記載したこれまでの理論と比較して、研究成果の価値や独自性を訴えます。ヘッジをうまく活用して、自分の議論の弱点を防御します。自分の研究の不備な点や、不足する情報を書くことで、客観性を示します。さらに、今後の研究課題の示唆（implications）を書くと論文の価値が高まります。

・References　参考文献

　参考にした研究ではなく、本文中に記載したものだけを書きます。特に書籍の引用の場合はページ番号を書くべきです。これらは主張を裏付ける証拠となるので正確に記載します。

・Appendix / Appendices　付表

　研究の再現性を示すために、実験などに使った資料や、本文中に記載できなかった図表をもれなく書きます。

Task 2

次の各文は就職活動におけるジェンダー問題を調査した論文の Abstract です。下線の上に、Abstract の Introduction, Method, Result, Discussion のどれに該当するか記入しなさい。また、その理由を述べなさい。さらに、適切な順に並べ替えた場合に該当する記号を（　　）に記入しなさい。

a.　<u>Introduction</u>
This paper investigates the relatively poor status of women in the Japanese business world. The focus is on unequal opportunities in recruiting activities by major companies.
理由：＿＿＿＿＿＿＿＿＿＿＿＿＿＿＿＿＿＿＿＿＿＿＿＿＿＿＿＿＿＿＿

b.　＿＿＿＿＿＿＿＿＿＿＿＿
This paper suggests introducing gender equality recognition beginning in the early stages of education, such as the primary school level.
理由：＿＿＿＿＿＿＿＿＿＿＿＿＿＿＿＿＿＿＿＿＿＿＿＿＿＿＿＿＿＿＿

c.　＿＿＿＿＿＿＿＿＿＿＿＿
The results indicate that although attention is paid to providing equal job opportunities, there exist several obstacles to improving the current situation. For example, some arduous job routines could be inappropriate for female employees, and male workers are reluctant to take child leave.
理由：＿＿＿＿＿＿＿＿＿＿＿＿＿＿＿＿＿＿＿＿＿＿＿＿＿＿＿＿＿＿＿

d.　＿＿＿＿＿＿＿＿＿＿＿＿
To achieve this research objective, qualitative interviews were conducted with 30 individual recruitment officers at companies listed in the first section of the Tokyo Stock Exchange.
理由：＿＿＿＿＿＿＿＿＿＿＿＿＿＿＿＿＿＿＿＿＿＿＿＿＿＿＿＿＿＿＿

・適切な順番：**a** →（　　）→（　　）→（　　）

Task for Output 1

Task 2 の英文を読んで、「どうすれば男性の育児休暇の取得が増えるか」という課題に対しての解決方法を 1 つのパラグラフでまとめてください。 ▶ **Template 11** [p. 76]

Self-editing

1. 英文に結束ができているか確認しなさい。
2. 適切にヘッジやブースターが使われているか確認しなさい。

Peer Review: Make some comments.

1. ペアの英文の Self-editing を確認しなさい。
2. ペアの英文を読んで、短いコメントを書きなさい。

Writing Strategy 33 Writing Introduction of Research Paper

Introduction は研究論文を読んでもらうための一番大切な章です。特定の Move を作り、研究の設計図を示します。

Introduction で研究論文の全体像を示す

イントロダクションには大きく分けて下の表のように 3 つの Move があります。それぞれに活用するストラテジーがありますが、これはすべて読者が読む観点に立って記載します。ここを読めば研究の概要や成果が簡単にわかるように書きます。この章の完成度が低いと、論文を読む人は内容に関して興味を失います。

Move	目的	Writing Strategy	読者が読む観点
1	・研究領域を定義 ・重要性を訴求	主要な研究を引用 ブースターの活用	十分に先行研究をレヴューしているか
2	・研究ニッチの明示 ・検証されていない課題の提示	先行研究の問題を指摘	十分新規的な内容で興味深いか
3	・研究成果の価値の訴求 ・独自の研究課題 （以下必要に応じて） ・結果の示唆 ・論文の構成を提示	課題の対処方法を明示 結果を予告 議論の順番を示す	研究課題は重要か、端的に述べているか

☐ Move 1 の書き方

ここでは、論文を書くための十分な準備ができていることを示します。つまり研究分野の先行研究を確実に読みこなして、研究領域への理解や重要な最新の課題を認識していることを読者に訴えます。このためには以下のポイントが大切です。

1. 研究領域や分野が明確か ⇒ 研究課題を明示

2. 先行研究を十分読みこなしているか ⇒ 重要な研究を引用

3. 書く課題やテーマの重要性をしっかりとアピールしているか ⇒ ブースターを活用

■ *Group Work:* Ask the following questions to your classmates.

1. How many books and academic papers related to your major have you read?

2. What are important books in your main subject or interest?

3. Why do you think they are important?

Task for Output 2

上の質問の答えを参考に、自分の専門の中で一番重要だと思う本について書きなさい。なぜそれが重要だと思うのかも書きなさい。

The most important book in my field is _____

_____

_____

_____

_____

_____

Writing Strategy *34* Writing Move 1 in Your Introduction

- ・リサーチペーパーは evidence based で記述します。
- ・Move 1 のはじめに先行研究を利用して研究課題の重要性を述べます。
- ・時制を効果的に使い重要性を強調します。

□ リサーチペーパーは evidence based で記述します。

　研究の報告は常に客観的でなくてはなりません。自分の主張や議論には、必ず誰もが納得する根拠を示す必要があります。そのために<u>先行研究を引用しながら議論を進めていきます</u>。このため重要な研究をできるだけ多く読み、その内容を把握し、<u>critical thinking</u> をしておかなければなりません。

▶ **Chapter 6, Writing Strategy 19** [p. 50]

　なお、引用の書き方はこの章の Focus on Accuracy を参照してください。

□ Move 1 のはじめに先行研究を利用して研究課題の重要性を述べます。

　重要性の訴求には、Chapter 5 の Writing Strategy 15（p. 39）で学んだブースター表現を活用します。イントロダクションでよく使われる表現として、以下のような5つのタイプのブースターが使われます。いずれも研究課題が重要であることの根拠になります。

　1. 範囲の広さ：広く認められている研究領域である

　2. 数の多さ：研究の数が多い

　3. 期間の長さ：長い間取り組まれているテーマである

　4. 新規性：最新の研究領域である

　5. ポジティブさ：ポジティブな表現で強調する

　なお、詳細は Writing Tip by Corpus Analysis 3（p. 119）を参照してください。

□ 時制を効果的に使い重要性を強調します。

　先行研究を引用する際に使われる時制には以下のような特徴があります。

- ・現在時制：書き手の立場と同じ主張を裏付ける研究
- ・現在完了：複数の研究者が認識している客観的な研究
- ・過去時制：一過性のもので、書き手は特にその研究を支持はしていない

　なお、詳細は Chapter 14 の Focus on Accuracy（p. 127）を参照してください。

Task 3

次の各文は Writing Strategy 34 の 5 つのタイプのブースターのどれが使われているでしょうか。該当箇所に下線を引き、空所に最も適切なブースターの番号を記入しなさい。

a. Researchers have recently considered the effect on child education of volunteer activities for blind people.　　　　　　　　　　　　　　　　　　　[　　]

b. A number of studies have been conducted in the research field on the effects of employment among people with disabilities.　　　　　　　　　[　　]

c. It has been widely acknowledged that we need to enhance support for persons who are physically challenged.　　　　　　　　　　　　　　　[　　]

d. Research on reading disorders and dyslexia has long been conducted in Europe.
　　　　　　　　　　　　　　　　　　　　　　　　　　　　　[　　]

e. Providing equal opportunity has been an essential part of social studies. [　　]

Task for Output 3

次は障がいを持った人の雇用問題に関する論文のイントロダクションの Move 1 です。

Equal Opportunity

 DL 32　CD32

　Initial research into the labor market situation for disabled people sought to identify appropriate types of jobs (Brown, 1985; Fillmore, 1987). The researchers assumed that finding suitable working conditions for workers with disabilities could be reasonable solutions. Since then, numerous studies have identified the particular working environments for those people (e.g., Johnson, 1995; Palincsar, 2005). Questions have also been raised about how to involve private firms to provide suitable jobs for different types of disabilities. (Brillson, 2003; Rubic, 2010). Recent research has argued that developing relevant vocational education systems plays an important role in sustainable relationships with employers (McDonough, 2016; Penny, 2018). Many scholars point out the association between educational achievement and success in employment (e.g., Robinson, 2019). Therefore it is essential to explore the research on how to raise stakeholders' attention to disadvantages for disabled people in education and lifelong learning, and to improve such situations.

1. Writing Strategy 34 で学んだ項目が使用されている箇所に下線を引き、どのような効果があるのかその下に書きなさい。この章と次の章の Focus on Accuracy も参考にしてください。
2. グループで答えを確認しなさい。

▪ *Write It Down*

あなたのまわりや、新聞などの資料で障がいのある方の雇用の課題について調べ、それに対する解決案をノートに英文でまとめてください。 ▶ **Template 11** [p. 76]

▪ *Self-editing*

読みやすい英文か確認しなさい。

▪ *Peer Review:* Make some comments.

ペアの英文を読んでコメントを書きなさい。

Task for Output 4

自分の研究テーマに関する論文を活用してイントロダクションの Move 1 を書きなさい。

◼ *Self-editing*

Move 1 のストラテジーを十分に使っているか確認しなさい。

先行研究の引用方法と時制

■ これまでの研究を論文に引用する時は、研究者名とその論文や著書の発表年数を記載することで示します。

 Owen (2017)：Owen が 2017 年に発表した研究成果

■ 同じ著者が同年に複数の成果を発表している時は、次のように古い順に年号の後にアルファベットをつけて区別します。

 Owen (2016a)...Owen (2016b)

 なお、一つの文に記載する際は、Owen (2016a, 2016b) となります。

■ 文末などで引用する時は研究者名も（　　）の中に入れます。

 ... (Owen, 2016a)

■ 2つ以上の研究を（　　　）の中に並べる場合は、間にセミコロンを入れます。順番は、研究者名のアルファベット順に記載します。

 ...（Owen, 2017; Wilson, 2008）

■ 引用には文中に入れる統合引用（integrated-citation）と、文末にまとめる非統合引用（non-integrated-citation）の2種類があります。

1. Charles (2008) recognizes the importance of qualitative data analysis in the field of motivation.
2. The importance of qualitative data analysis in the field of motivation is identified (Charles, 2008).

・ 1のように統合引用を使う場合、その研究自体に焦点を当てていることになります。書き手が主観的に、自分の論文の中で重要な位置を占める研究と考えて引用します。

・ 2のような非統合引用の場合は、記述した内容が一般に客観的な事実として認識されていると考え、その根拠となる研究として文末に記載します。

Writing Tip by Corpus Analysis 3
— リサーチペーパーでよく使われるブースター表現

研究領域やテーマの重要性を読者に訴える際に以下の表現がよく活用されます。

1. 範囲の広さ：広く認められている研究領域である

It is widely believed that ...　　広く信じられている

It is generally assumed that ...　　一般に想定されている

It is well known that ...　　よく知られている

2. 数の多さ：研究の数が多い

A number of studies have been conducted ...　　研究が多数行われている

Many researchers have argued that ...　　研究者が多数議論している

Numerous research projects have pointed out ...　　多くの研究が指摘している

3. 期間の長さ：長い間取り組まれているテーマである

There is a long tradition of research within ...　　長い伝統がある

... research has long been recognized that ...　　長期間認識されている

... studies over several decades have shown that ...　　数十年の示唆がある

4. 新規性：最新の研究領域である

Recent research trends towards ...　　最新の研究の傾向では

Researchers have recently considered ...　　研究者が最新と考えている

Current theory suggests that ...　　最新の理論が示唆している

5. ポジティブさ：ポジティブな表現で強調する

There is compelling evidence that ...　　説得力のある証拠がある

... is no longer open to doubt ...　　疑いの余地がない

A central concern in the study of ...　　研究の中心的関心事である

... has been an essential part of ...　　必須の分野である

... have been extremely successful ...　　とても成功している

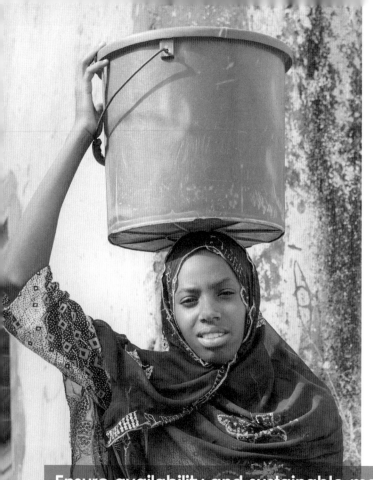

Topic: Clean Water for Everyone

6 CLEAN WATER AND SANITATION

Ensure availability and sustainable management of water and sanitation for all.

Chapter 14
Creating a Research Niche

■ **Pre-Task :** Talk with your classmates about importance of water supply in developing countries.

☑ **Strategic Points** ⋯ Introduction Move 2: Creating a research niche
Introduction Move 3: Occupying the niche

This chapter deals with how to develop a persuasive essay.

▶ この章で学ぶこと ▶研究論文の書き方の基礎
▶研究の独自性の明示方法

Strategic Focus 14: Importance of Your Research

研究の独自性と、論文の価値の伝え方を学びます。

─Task 1─

次の質問についてクラスメイトと話し合い、自分の考えを書きなさい。

1. What are important points when reading research articles?

_____

_____

2. What is originality in research?

_____

_____

Writing Strategy 35 Creating a Research Niche

論文の新規性と独自性

研究論文には新規性や独自性が必要です。研究とは特定の研究領域でまだ解明されていない課題に取り組み、あらたな価値を提示することです。つまり、自分が書くトピックに関してこれまでに行われた研究をすべて確認し、新しいテーマを見つけることです。これは研究のニッチ（niche）と呼ばれ、論文では先行研究の問題点を指摘して記述します。ニッチを読者に明確に伝えるのがIntroduction の Move 2 です。

以下が代表的な文の書き出しです。

・There is little research ...　　There are few studies ...

すべての論文を調べた確信がない場合は、次のようにヘッジを活用してディフェンスします。

▶ **Chapter 5, Writing Strategy 14** [p. 38]

・There **seems to** be little research ...　**To my knowledge**, there are few studies ...

□ ニッチの作り方

ニッチの5つの観点から、先行研究で行われていない点を指摘する方法があります。

   1. サンプル：実験や調査の対象者や対象物

   2. 実験などの条件：データを集めた時間、季節、場所

   3. 実験タスクとデータの収集方法：実験に使用したタスク、データの収集方法

4. 分析の方法：収集したデータの分析手法
5. 理論やモデルに基づく解釈：分析結果の解釈を行う背景となる理論

・先行研究を読むときはこの5つのニッチの観点から批判的に読みこなします。
　　例 「なぜ当該研究は5つの観点から研究を行い、なぜそれが妥当だと言えるのか。」

Task 2

次の各文は Writing Strategy 35 の1～5のニッチのどれを活用して先行研究の問題を指摘しているでしょうか。空所にニッチの番号を記入しなさい。また、該当する箇所に下線を引きなさい。

a. However, since their observation analysis only deals with a short period, it is important to examine water pollution effects over a longer period. 　　　[　　　]

b. However, versions of these models suffer from intractable problems. 　[　　　]

c. However, there has been little attention to the potential for AI data analyses.
　　　　　　　　　　　　　　　　　　　　　　　　　　　　　　　　[　　　]

d. Although a number of interview and observation methods have been conducted, few studies have used a reliable questionnaire for data collection. 　[　　　]

e. However, there is little research which investigates whether this water sanitation system can be effective in African nations. 　　　　　　　　　　[　　　]

Task for Output 1

以下は水資源の問題に関する論文の Introduction の一部です。

Clean Water Issues

🎧 DL 33　💿 CD 33

It has been reported that water and sanitation services are severely lacking in developing countries (Adams, 2015; Bishop, 2016). More than 2.6 billion people live without proper services for access to water and sanitation (WHO, 2015). James (2018) points out that every year millions of poor people die from preventable diseases. The main victims are women and children. Although numerous potential solutions have been proposed, there seems to be little research which provides concrete evidence for long term benefits of new schemes. As Sharp (2019) claims, few studies have reported on practical theories to improve difficulties caused by the lack of local government will and lack of investment for maintaining services.

1. 研究のニッチの個所に下線を引き、どのような観点からそれを使っているのか書きなさい。
2. グループで答えを確認しなさい。

■ *Write It Down*

水資源の具体的な課題を調べて記述しなさい。発展途上国におけるものでも構いません。問題の原因と、どのような状況で何が起こっているのかをノートに英文で簡単にまとめましょう。

■ *Self-editing*

読みやすい英文か確認しなさい。

■ *Peer Review:* Make some comments.

ペアの英文を読んでコメントを書きなさい。

Writing Strategy **36** Occupying the Niche

Introduction の Move 3 では、Move 2 で示した研究のニッチをどのように解決するのか記述します。

Chapter 13 の Writing Strategy 33（p. 112）で示したように、主に次の3つの目的があります。

1. 研究の価値の訴求：Move 2 で指摘した課題の対処方法
2. 結果の示唆：主な研究結果を事前に提示
3. 論文の構成を提示：後に続く論文の構成の予告

研究の価値を訴求するために、Move 3 の書き出しは以下のような決まった表現が使われます。

Here we	present / report / perform / use
In this article we	present / report
This study	examines / investigates

書き出しの後には以下の表現がよく使われます。

To demonstrate this point ...   To achieve this goal ...

結果の示唆には次のような表現が多く使われます。

The results indicate ...   Our conclusions ...

論文の構成を提示するには、Writing Tip by Corpus Analysis 2（p. 36）で示した時間・順序を表すメタディスコースを使います。

First, Second, Then, Finally

Task for Output 2

以下は水資源の問題に関する論文のイントロダクションの Move 2 と 3 です。

 DL 34 CD34

The purpose of this article is to explore whether a recently developed slow sand filtration method could solve water and sanitation services in developing countries. Yamaha Motor Co. developed
5 the home use water purifier in 1991. The company started its clean water project when they set up a factory in a part of Indonesia where people

lived in areas without a clean water supply. The company commercially launched the slow sand filtration system. The unique aspect of their business model is to
10 form partnerships with a variety of different funding organizations which support developing countries. This study examines the effectiveness of their new water project and business schemes. To achieve this goal, we conducted interviews and observation studies with several stakeholders in eight different areas in developing countries. The results indicate that the eco-friendly and simple system has been
15 welcomed by the local communities. The attributes of their effective partnerships model could solve financial and long-term maintenance issues. In this paper, at first we review previous studies regarding water and sanitation problems in developing countries. Second, data collecting and analysis methods for the current interview and observation are presented. Then we show the results of the studies
20 in developing countries. Finally, we provide implications of our research findings.

1. Writing Strategy 36 で示した Move 3 に関連する表現に下線を引き、どのような観点からそれを使っているのか書きなさい。

2. グループで答えを確認しなさい。

◼ Write It Down

ここで示されている水資源問題の現状の課題とそれに対する解決方法についてどう思うか、ノートに英文で自分の意見を述べなさい。▶ Template 11 [p. 76]

◼ Self-editing

読みやすい英文か確認しなさい。

◼ Peer Review: Make some comments.

ペアの英文を読んでコメントを書きなさい。

Writing Your Introduction

Chapter 13 と、この章を参考に、Template 12 を活用して自分の研究に該当する Introduction を書きなさい。

Template 12 ■ Introduction of Research Paper

Move 1

Topic sentence

1) It is widely acknowledged ＿＿＿＿＿＿＿＿＿＿＿＿. （複数の研究を引用）

　　※ ブースターを選ぶ　　　　　研究領域と課題を書く

2) In particular, ＿＿＿＿＿＿＿＿＿＿＿. （重要な研究を引用）

　　　　　課題の中で重要な点を書く

3) For instance, ＿＿＿＿＿＿＿＿＿＿＿. （特に重要な研究）

　　　　　特に注目する研究課題

Move 2

1) However, there are few studies ＿＿＿＿＿＿＿＿＿＿＿＿＿＿＿＿.

　　※ ネガティブな表現

　　※ ニッチの観点 1 ～ 5 (Writing Strategy 35, p. 121) を選ぶ

2) Furthermore, ＿＿＿＿＿＿＿＿＿＿＿＿＿＿＿＿.

　　※ ニッチの観点 1 ～ 5 のより具体的な問題点

　　ニッチの数に応じて 1) → 2) を繰り返す

Move 3

1) In this paper ＿＿＿＿＿＿＿＿＿＿＿＿＿＿.

　　※ メタディスコース　　ニッチで提示した課題の解決方法

2) To do this ＿＿＿＿＿＿＿＿＿＿＿＿＿.

　　※ メタディスコース　　　具体的な対処法

　必要に応じて

　　　・結果の示唆

　　　・論文の構成の提示

Focus on Accuracy : Tense

時制

　時制は英文ライティングでもエラーの多い項目です。事象の伝達などでは、一般に過去に起こった事象は過去時制で報告し、現在のことは現在時制で表現します。しかし、エッセイや研究論文の目的は、書き手が読者に、調べた事項を報告したり、研究の成果を伝えたりすることです。

　時制は書き手と、伝える内容の時間的な距離の提示となります。また、この距離は時間だけでなく、伝達内容に対する書き手のスタンスも暗示しています。

　例えば現在時制は、伝達者の目の前に概念的に存在している事象を表現し、自分の主張としてそれにコミットしていることを表します。つまり書き手のスタンスに近いものに言及する時に使用されます。一方、過去時制は、伝達者との距離があり、過去の一時期に存在したもので、今はそれほど書き手の立場に影響を与えない事象を示すことが一般的です。

　論文の執筆において、2つの時制の概念があります。1つは言及している研究が行われた時点の出来事としての時制です。もう1つは、それを書き手が読者に伝える時点での時制です。前者の場合、既に行われた実験や分析に関する記述は、過去時制を使用すると考えられます。しかし、書き手がその事象にコミットし、自分の研究スタンスと近い場合や、自分の主張をサポートする際は、現在時制で表現されます。

　後者の書き手が読者に伝える時点の時制では、先行研究に対する評価や報告を行う際の単なる事象としての提示は、一般に過去時制を使います。さらに、先行研究に対してコミットしていない場合にも過去時制は使われます。

　反対に、報告内容の重要性を示し、自分の主張を支持するものとして引用する場合は、現在時制を使う傾向があります。また、複数の先行研究を引用し、書き手が自分の研究分野の重要性を訴える場合は、現在完了の時制が使われます。下の表のように、過去とそれ以外とを区別し、前者はコミットしていない状況、後者は書き手の研究スタンスに近いことを示すと考えます。

時制	出来事	報告
過去時制	・過去の一時点 ・今は異なる	・コミットしていない ・賛成はしない
現在時制	・現在の一時点 ・習慣や普遍の事象	・自分と同じスタンス ・普遍性がある
現在完了時制	・過去から始まり今も続いている事象	・複数の人も支持 ・客観性がある

Chapter 15
Review

■ **Pre-Task :** Talk with your classmates about important academic writing strategies.

☑ **Strategic Points** ⋯ Enhancing reader-centered strategies

This chapter reviews what we have learned about academic writing strategies.

▶ この章で学ぶこと　▶これまで学んだアカデミック・ライティングのストラテジーの復習

━Review 1 ━

Developing Cohesion and Coherence
次のパラグラフには読みやすさを実現するためにどのようなストラテジーが使われていますか。該当する箇所に下線を引き、説明を書きなさい。

 DL 35　CD35

　　Current online technologies have improved mobile phones to a great level for our daily life. With the help of mobile phones, it is possible to access various social media sites such as Facebook and Instagram. By using these sites, we can stay connected with our friends, family and many other people in the world. Also by using apps, we can watch videos and movies whenever we want. Additionally, we can make use of useful apps for news, health, and shopping. In sum, the mobile phone is a very important device which helps us in various ways in modern life.

▶ **Writing Strategies 1-15**

━Review 2 ━

Writing a Paragraph
Some people protest animal testing for developing cosmetics and medicines. Others claim it is a necessary step to obtain biological data. Describe your opinion.

1. Brainstorming で、できるだけたくさんの関連語彙を書きだしなさい。

・＿＿＿＿＿＿　・＿＿＿＿＿＿　・＿＿＿＿＿＿　・＿＿＿＿＿＿
・＿＿＿＿＿＿　・＿＿＿＿＿＿　・＿＿＿＿＿＿　・＿＿＿＿＿＿
・＿＿＿＿＿＿　・＿＿＿＿＿＿　・＿＿＿＿＿＿　・＿＿＿＿＿＿

2. Cluster map を作りなさい。

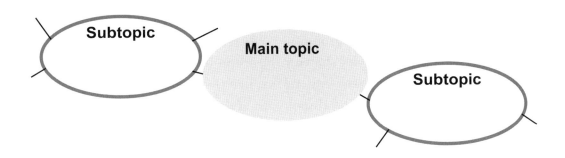

■ *Write It Down*

Cluster Map を活用してパラグラフを書きなさい。

_____

_____

_____

_____

_____

_____

_____

▶ **Writing Strategies 14-29**

━ *Review 3* ━

Writing a Paragraph

次の英文はある論文の Abstract です。どのような Move で構成されていますか。また、読みやすさ
を実現させるために、どのようなストラテジーが使われていますか。該当箇所に下線を引き、説明を
書きなさい。

⬇ DL 36 ◉ CD36

This study examines current patterns of oral communication strategy (OCS) use, to what degree these strategies can be explicitly taught, and the extent to which strategy can lead to improvements
5　in oral communication ability. In a twelve-week English as a Foreign Language (EFL) course based

on a communicative approach, sixty-two female learners were divided into two groups. The strategy training group (n = 28) received metacognitive training, focusing on OCS use, whereas the control group (n = 34) received only the
10　normal communicative course with no explicit focus on OCSs. The effects of the training were assessed using three types of data collection: the participants' pre- and post-course oral communication test scores, transcription data from the tests, and retrospective protocol data for their task performance. The findings revealed that participants in the strategy training group significantly improved
15　their oral proficiency test scores, whereas improvements in the control group were

not significant. The results of the transcription and retrospective protocol data analyses confirmed that the participants' success was partly due to an increased general awareness of OCSs and to the use of specific OCSs, such as maintenance of fluency and negotiation of meaning, to solve interactional difficulties.

▶ **Writing Strategy 32**

━ *Review 4* ━

Writing Introduction

次の英文はある論文の Introduction です。どのような Move で構成されていますか。また、読みやすさを実現させるためどのようなストラテジーが使われていますか。該当箇所に下線を引き、説明を書きなさい。　　　　🎧 DL 37　◎ CD37

　　Numerous attempts have been made by researchers to show the effects of learning strategies on target language (TL) development (e.g., Cohen, Weaver, & Li, 1998; O'Malley & Chamot, 1990; Oxford, 1996; Rubin, 1975). Learning strategies are the conscious thoughts and behaviors used by learners to help them better
5　understand, learn, and remember the TL information.
　　Researchers also recognize that learners can improve their communicative ability by developing learning strategies that enable them to become independent learners of the TL (Dadour & Robbins, 1996; Labarca & Khanji, 1986), reflecting the widely held belief that strategies for communication relate to successful
10　language performance (e.g., Dörnyei, 1995; Huang & Naerssen, 1987; Rost & Ross, 1991). The main reason is that the use of communication strategy (CS) can solve communicative disruptions and enhance interaction in the TL (Dörnyei & Scott, 1997; Faerch & Kasper, 1983a; Tarone, 1980). In particular, the role of specific strategies such as negotiation of meaning has been an important object of study for
15　a long time (e.g., Long, 1983; Pica, 2002; Varonis & Gass, 1985). However, most of these studies were conducted in experimental settings and only a few studies have explored second language (L2) learners' actual CS use in classroom contexts (Foster, 1998; Williams, Inscoe, & Tasker, 1997). We should not overlook Foster's (1998) claim that there is little research that has demonstrated a direct relationship
20　between the incidence of strategies for negotiation and an increase in language proficiency in classroom contexts. Additionally, the majority of negotiation research has not included other types of CSs, such as using fillers or shadowing, as communication enhancers for maintaining and developing TL discourse. As Williams et al. (1997) argued, learners also need to use such strategies to develop
25　their interaction in actual communicative contexts; thus, it is worthwhile to

examine the effects of such strategy use.

Another problematic issue is that the research in interlanguage (IL) negotiation has analyzed learners' interaction by a single method—transcription data analysis—which makes it difficult to interpret learners' actual intention of specific
5 strategy use. Researchers claim that the nature of the available data on strategies depends on the collection method, and there seems to be no fully established set of assessment procedures yet (Cohen, 1998; O'Malley & Chamot, 1990). Therefore, to compensate for problems inherent in the single method, it is essential to introduce multiple data collection procedures to obtain more accurate and valid data on
10 learners' cognitive processes and strategy use. By combining several assessment methods, this study addresses the question of whether the use of CSs that include not only negotiation of meaning but also communication enhancers can develop English as a foreign language (EFL) learners' oral proficiency in classroom settings. Sixty-two Japanese college students participated in a 12-week course of
15 English lessons based on a communicative approach with explicit strategy training. They had a conversation test before and after the training. I transcribed the post-training test to analyze whether participants' actual strategy use, production rates, and the number of errors have an effect on students' TL development. As a reliable questionnaire method, this study used the Oral Communication Strategy
20 Inventory (OCSI), which was developed by using factor analysis based on a survey of 400 Japanese students (Nakatani, 2006). Additionally, the participants reviewed their task performance by listening to the audiotape recorded during the conversation test and provided a retrospective think-aloud protocol. I also transcribed these data and examined participants' awareness of specific strategy
25 usage. Although this triangulated approach revealed a slight difference among the results of respective analyses, I suggest that the use of specific CSs for interaction could improve EFL learners' oral proficiency.

▶ **Writing Strategies 31-34**

本書にはCD（別売）があります

Academic Writing Strategies

Focus on Global Issues for Sustainable Development Goals

大学生のためのアカデミックライティング・ストラテジー

2020年1月20日　初版第1刷発行
2024年2月20日　初版第8刷発行

著　者　　中 谷　安 男

発行者　　福 岡　正 人

発行所　　株式会社　**金 星 堂**

（〒101-0051）　東京都千代田区神田神保町 3-21
Tel　　（03）3263-3828（営業部）
　　　　（03）3263-3997（編集部）
Fax　　（03）3263-0716
https://www.kinsei-do.co.jp

編集担当　松本明子・西田碧　　　　　Printed in Japan
印刷所／日新印刷株式会社　製本所／松島製本
ISBN978-4-7647-4109-6　C1082